Bail Bonds 201, written by veteran bail agent Sean Cook, imparts a wealth of knowledge and provides the reader with the tools to exercise sound judgment in the bail bond business. The wisdom shared is borne from real bail bonding situations that will help the novice and veteran alike avoid mistakes that can be devastating to anyone engaged in the industry. Mr. Cook, who also authored "Bail Bonds 101," tells of his own real-life bail experiences, as well as the wisdom he gained in seeking out information and guidance from other bail agents that have succeeded -- and failed – in the business. Each chapter includes a section entitled, "Warning Signs," which details situations that invariably arise as a retail bail agent and then offers an approach and specific suggestions for dealing with specific circumstances so that proper judgment is exercised.

As the time-tested adage tells us: "Good judgment comes from experience, and experience comes with bad judgment." Everyone in the bail bond business – and anyone thinking about entering the business – can gain from the experience passed on by Mr. Cook and will undoubtedly find "Bail Bonds 201" to be an indispensable resource of what to do -- and what not to do -- to exercise good judgment in a retail bail bond agency.

Brian J. Frank
Lexington National Insurance Corp.

Bail Bonds 201

Insider Tips to Avoiding Common Mistakes and Pitfalls of the Bail Industry

Sean M. Cook

NOTES TO THE READER:

The information presented in this book was obtained by the author through personal experience and through sources the author considers reliable and reputable. The author's purpose in writing this book is to explain the reasons why many bail companies fail. While the author believes that taking the recommended precautions will help Bail Company owners avoid common mistakes, following the steps presented in this book is not a guaranteed prescription for success. The author disclaims any liability, loss or risk taken by individuals who act, either directly or indirectly, on the information presented in this book.

The pronoun "he" is used for convenience in this book to refer indistinctly to male and female bail agents.

The material discussed in this book assumes a basic understanding of how the bail industry works. For a more general discussion of the bail industry, please refer to *Bail Bonds 101: The Complete Guide to Owning and Operating a Successful Bail Bond Company* by Sean M. Cook (Huntington Beach, CA: Bail Out Publishing 2005, ISBN: 0-9764958-0-5).

ISBN 0-9764958-1-3
Bail Out Publishing, Huntington Beach CA

CONTENTS

1

WHY DO BAIL BOND COMPANIES FAIL?

If you have ever driven near a courthouse, police station or jail, particularly in an urban area, you have probably seen plenty of advertisements for bail bond agencies. Open your local yellow pages and you will see even more. Bail bond services seem to be in high demand. As a result, new bail bond agencies open all the time. If you are hoping to break into the bail industry, it shouldn't surprise you that you will be facing competition. What might surprise you is how frequently the names on those bail bond ads will change over time.

Many new bail agencies go out of business within their first year, primarily because they make critical mistakes that lead to bad decisions and bigger mistakes. When the difficulties snowball into failure, the new bail bond agent is forced to close his doors.

The good news is that with the knowledge you will gain from this book and some careful planning on your part, you can avoid the common mistakes that trap many new bail agents. If you take the appropriate steps and make a commitment to grow your business slowly and steadily, based on sound decisions, you can create a successful bail bond company and enjoy longevity in a lucrative industry.

In this book, I will discuss the typical reasons bail bond companies fail and give you tips on how to avoid these common mistakes. I'll explain how a few little mistakes can lead to big problems and discuss how to avoid or correct the resulting difficulties. Since every big problem in the bail bond business stems from small mistakes, you can take specific measures to avoid these problems or correct mistakes before they grow out of control.

Reading this book once is not enough. Creating a successful bail bond agency is an ongoing project that requires continuous effort and diligence. Trouble has a way of sneaking up on you, but if you put the right systems into place, create a series of self-checks and continually review and reevaluate your decisions, you'll be able to build a successful bail company that lasts.

While this book is primarily a resource for new bail agents or bail agents trying to determine why their business is in trouble, it is also a valuable reference for any small business owner. Many of the problem areas discussed in this book are common among small businesses in any industry. The bail agent is vulnerable to risk and liability beyond what most business owners encounter. Therefore, the bail industry offers the ultimate example of what can go wrong in any business and how to avoid it. If you learn how a bail agent minimizes risk and keeps his business out of trouble, you can apply these principles to any small business.

Overview

To gain the most from this book, it will help if you already have a working knowledge of how the bail industry operates.[1] But let's go through a quick overview so it will be easier to see where problems arise.

The bail agent's job is to post bail for a defendant who has been arrested. Bail represents the defendant's promise that he will show up in court when required. To back that promise, the defendant or a cosigner usually presents the bail agent with collateral sufficient to cover the amount of bail. To compensate the bail agent for performing his job, the defendant or cosigner pays a premium, which is a percentage of the bail amount – 10% in most states. After the bail bond is posted, the defendant is released from jail, awaiting his court appearances. When all court appearances are completed, the judge exonerates the bail and the bail agent's case is closed. That's how bail is supposed to work.

Unfortunately the bail process doesn't always go according to plan. If the defendant does not show up in court – if he skips town – the bail bond is forfeited. This means the bail agent either has to track down the defendant and have him rearrested, or pay the bail himself – and then go about the task of collecting on the collateral the defendant or his cosigner had posted.

Too many forfeitures can mean the end of your bail business. Here's why:

---

[1] If you need an introductory guide or a refresher, please refer to *Bail Bonds 101: The Complete Guide to Owning and Operating a Successful Bail Bond Company* by Sean M. Cook (Huntington Beach, CA: Bail Out Publishing 2005, ISBN: 0-9764958-0-5).

- You'll spend too much time, effort and money trying to make up for the loss – or trying to track down a defendant that skipped.
- You'll have to depend on the cosigner's collateral to cover the amount of the forfeited bond, and if the collateral is not sufficient, you will be out the amount you have to pay to cover the bail.
- The surety company that backs your business and pays the court for any forfeited bail that you are unable to cover might refuse to let you write new bail. At the very least, you will be in debt to the surety company until you have reimbursed them for the amount of bail they paid on your behalf, and they will keep you under close scrutiny.

Though forfeitures are always a risk in the bail industry, if you plan your business well, you can minimize your risk:

- By avoiding the most common mistakes that lead to forfeitures.
- By not overreacting when a forfeiture comes along, thereby making even bigger mistakes that lead to bigger risks and therefore increasing the probability of more forfeitures down the road.

Common mistakes

In the chapters that follow, I will explain the most common mistakes that lead to forfeitures and, ultimately, to the failure of a bail bond company:

- Bailing out the wrong people.
- Failing to complete due diligence.
- Trying to grow too quickly.
- Letting work pile up.
- Limiting availability.
- Failing to write a business plan.

Any one of these mistakes can be enough to cause trouble for a new bail agent if the mistake isn't caught and fixed quickly. But often a new bail agent makes more than one mistake at the same time, and the problems overlap and escalate. The good news is that by fixing one mistake, you will often minimize the chances of making further mistakes. Each chapter in this book is devoted to a discussion of one of these common mistakes, focused around the following questions:

1. Where does the trouble usually start?
2. What are the warning signs?
3. How do you get out of trouble and avoid problems in the future?

As you read this book, you'll discover that these common mistakes arise from one of three reasons:

- *Too much ambition* – You try to grow your business too quickly or write too much "big" bail, thereby incurring unnecessary risk. When this risk catches up to you and puts your business in financial jeopardy, you will be tempted to write even bigger bail to attempt to dig yourself out of the hole – increasing your risk further.

- *Too little planning or organization* – You advertise and write bail without giving enough thought to a business plan, a budget and a timetable for growth. Before long you find it difficult to keep up with your operating expenses, e.g., advertising costs, rent for office space, and employee salaries. Or you find yourself falling behind in your paperwork, failing to collect payments owed to you and losing track of your open cases. You unwittingly skip critical steps in the due diligence process that you should be conducting with every new client. Each of these mistakes puts you further at risk, and the problems escalate.

- *Desperation* – You write bail because you desperately need the money to keep up with your expenses or to make up for your loss on a bond that was forfeited. Desperation results in carelessness and lack of due diligence. In short you write bail to earn the premium and not because the defendant is a good risk. The problems continue to grow from there.

As you can see, these pitfalls often overlap. One leads to another in a vicious circle. If you try to grow your bail bond business too quickly, for example, you will focus on writing as much bail as possible rather than setting out a budget and a plan for slow, steady growth. As a result, you might become overextended on your advertising or office space expenses and find it difficult to keep up with your payments. The vicious circle continues. Because you worry that you won't meet your expenses at the end of the month, you are tempted to write bigger bail at a faster pace. You ignore precautions. You don't perform the proper due diligence on a defendant or you accept insufficient collateral from a cosigner. The trouble then snowballs out of control. The bail is forfeited, you lose money and perhaps the backing of your surety company, and soon you are out of business.

The vicious circle looks like this:

A bail agent in trouble will be caught in this circle, where one problem leads to another, around and around or back and forth. Reaction to one problem causes another problem. If the bail agent stays caught in this circle too long, the result will be too many forfeitures and ultimately the end of his bail business.

Focus on success

As a new bail agent, your best success strategy is to carefully avoid these problem areas and the mistakes that result. The rest of this book will provide guidance on how to avoid common mistakes. You'll discover that the best rule of thumb is to *focus on writing good bail for the right reasons* and resolve to grow your business at a steady, organized pace. If you create a solid business plan, stick to it, keep your ambition in check, stay organized, and avoid carelessness and desperation you can have a very successful bail bond company. This book will help you learn how to think and plan your way through any problems that arise. The last thing you want to do is react to an obstacle without thinking the causes and consequences through. If you feel that you are becoming desperate to write bigger bail ask yourself, *why*? Is it because you've overextended on your advertising or office space and have too many bills to pay? Is it because you already owe money on a previous forfeiture? Keeping the cause in mind, what can you do to improve the situation without creating more trouble?

You should always answer these questions carefully before you address any problem, so you won't be tempted to make increasingly bad decisions that can cost you hundreds of thousands of dollars, not to mention your career. Careful thought and planning is the best way to stay out of the vicious circle that leads many bail agencies to fail. The more time you take to make wise decisions and stay on top of all the bail you write, the more likely you are to succeed with your bail bond company and enjoy a rewarding and profitable career.

2

BAILING OUT THE RIGHT PEOPLE

As a bail agent, your business success depends on the bail you write. If you write good bail, for which the defendant meets his obligations to the court and the bail is ultimately exonerated, you can have a rewarding business. If you write risky bail, you are more likely to experience more trouble than success.

Writing good bail requires assessing risk versus reward, which boils down to bailing out the right people for the right reasons. If you don't, you'll end up chasing down skips (defendants that defaulted their obligation) and paying forfeitures. Exposing yourself deliberately to forfeitures is not a good business strategy. Higher-risk bonds might seem lucrative, in terms of your premium. But higher-risk bonds are more likely to expose you to forfeitures, and you risk owing a greater amount to the court if the defendant skips. This means a risky bond can cost you more in the long run than the premium you earned.

What are the costs of a forfeiture?

1. The cost of tracking down the defendant.
2. The cost of paying the bond amount if the defendant isn't found.

9

3. The risk of losing your surety company backing.

Because forfeitures are one of the fastest ways for a bail agency to go out of business, it's important to examine the danger of forfeitures in more detail.

The danger of forfeitures

Forfeitures are perhaps the single biggest reason bail agencies fail. Forfeitures are typically an indication that the bail agent is more focused on the 10% premium than on the potential risk. If too many defendants are skipping, the bail agent is not following the sound business practice of writing good low-risk bail backed by a careful practice of due diligence. Instead, the bail agent is writing risky bail in order to earn more premiums. When reward becomes more important than risk, trouble awaits.

Don't focus on the premium

A bail bond represents more than the premium you earn. It represents a liability in the full amount of the bond. It's as if you've written a check for the defendant to pay the full amount of bail, and you are left to trust that he will fulfill his obligations to the court, so the bail can be exonerated. If not, you will be left to pay the forfeited amount.

When you start focusing on the premium you can earn, you start to ignore the liability. If you write bail just for the amount you can earn to cover your business expenses, you are playing a numbers game. You have to decide – is the premium you will earn worth more than the risk of writing this bond? The risk, remember, is that the defendant will skip, leaving you to pay the forfeiture.

While this premium might solve your current expense problems, what kinds of problems will you have if this defendant skips? Are you certain this is a good bond to write… for the *right* reasons?

Forfeitures catch up all at once

The biggest problem with forfeitures is that they often catch up to you all at once. If you are just starting out in the bail business, several years might pass without any forfeitures coming into play. Why? Because the defendants for whom you wrote the bail are still in court. Cases often take months, sometimes years to resolve. Meanwhile, you continue to write more bail, increasing your liability with each new bond.

Several years later, one of your earlier defendants might be wrapping up his court case. At the start of the case, he believed he would be acquitted, but the tide has turned and now he faces the prospect of a guilty verdict. The likelihood of his serving serious prison time increases. Rather than take his chances on the verdict, he skips – leaving you with the forfeited bond.

The cost of forfeitures

Every time a defendant skips, it will cost you time and money to track him down. If you hire a bounty hunter to help you locate the skip, most of the premium you earned on the bond, if not more, will go to pay the bounty hunter's fees.

If you don't find the skip, you will be responsible for paying the bond amount to the court. You'll have to pay the amount yourself or go into debt with your surety company. Then you'll need to convert the defendant's collateral into equity in order to reimburse yourself or the surety company – assuming you have sufficient collateral and that it's really worth what the defendant claimed.

The risk of losing your surety backing

If you have too many forfeitures, your surety company might refuse to back you any longer. They can put you temporarily on hold and refuse to issue additional bonds. Or they can pull all your paperwork, cancel your contract and tell you that you can't write bail for them any longer.

Why? Remember that the surety company is the first point of liability on a bail bond. They back each bond you write. They are responsible for paying the forfeited bond amount to the court if you don't have the amount available in your Build-Up Fund (BUF) account or bank account. A surety company does not want to increase its risk by backing an agent that consistently writes bad bail or high-risk bail. An excessive number of forfeitures signals to the surety company that you are not writing good bail. You are a risk to them and to yourself.

While they might not cancel your contract over just the one forfeited bond, if you've been writing bad bonds all along, that forfeiture is just the first one of many that will start to hit, one after another. If you have too many forfeitures, even if you have collateral to cover them, there's a good chance your surety company will cut you off permanently. You won't be able to write bail under their auspices any longer, because you've increased their liability too much and become too great of a risk. You've demonstrated to them that you do not consistently write good bail.

When a bail agent is dropped by a surety company, that agent can usually find another surety company to back him. If the agent starts running into more forfeitures, however, the new surety company will drop him too. Meanwhile, the agent is still obligated to reimburse the surety company for any forfeitures paid on his behalf. The surety company might also have a lien on the agent's house. With that type of financial pressure, it's going to require a great deal of discipline to keep from repeating the same mistake over and over: writing risky bonds to earn greater premiums.

18 bonds to pay off one forfeiture

It's an industry rule of thumb that *it takes 18 bonds of an equal amount to pay off one forfeited bond.*

If you write a $10,000 bond today and the bond is forfeited, you will need to write 18 more $10,000 bonds to pay off the forfeited bond. You'll need that many more premiums just to cover the forfeited amount, plus the expense of tracking down the skip. When you keep this rule in mind, the $1,000 premium on one risky bond no longer seems attractive. It would be hard enough to write 18 bonds in the amount of $10,000 each, to make up for one forfeit. What if the forfeited bond was for $100,000? You'd have to write 18 more $100,000 bonds to cover the loss. That's very hard to do, and every one of those bonds entails another $100,000 liability. When you feel pressured to pay off a forfeited bond, you might fall into the trap of making more bad decisions to get the next 20 bonds written quickly, thereby increasing your risk of more forfeitures. The numbers game doesn't work very well in the bail industry. One bad $100,000 bond can put you out of business or in debt to your surety company for years. How do you avoid this trouble? By knowing where it starts, and by creating a successful business strategy that allows you to focus on writing profitable yet lower-risk bonds.

Where does the trouble start?

Why do bail agents get into trouble with forfeitures? The trouble starts when they base their bail decisions on criteria other than the stability and reliability of the defendant and cosigner – verified by solid background checks – and confirmation of sufficient collateral. Good bail means that you have a good feeling about the defendant and cosigner, and you perform the due diligence necessary to confirm your feelings. If the situation doesn't look good and you write the bail anyway, you're not writing good bail. You're putting yourself at risk for forfeitures. Most bail agents run into problems when they start basing their bail decisions not on the proper criteria, but on an immediate need for cash flow. Because they have overhead expenses to pay they don't want to turn away a potential premium. They never know when another client will come along or how high the next bail bond will be. Therefore they are tempted to write every bond that comes through the door regardless of whether or not it is a good risk. They also know that since their premium rate is fixed by state regulations, the larger the bond they write, the more income they will earn. Thus they base their decision on the dollar amount of the bond, rather than the soundness of the risk.

The danger here is twofold: Not only do they ignore the need for risk assessment but also the fact that the larger bonds ($100,000 versus $1,000) carry much higher liability in case of a forfeiture (remember the rule of thumb: a bail agent would need to write approximately 18 bonds in the same amount to cover the loss).

Despite the obvious risks of writing bad bail, it's surprising how quickly the premium becomes a ruling factor in bail decisions. Agents bail out the wrong people – individuals that are obviously bad bail risks – because they are desperate for premiums. When considering whether or not to write a bail bond, too often the bail agent asks, "How badly do I need this premium right now?" rather than, "Is this defendant a good risk?" As a surety professional once told me, "The aroma of the premium outweighs the stench of the forfeitures."

Fortunately, you can avoid this problem by paying attention to the warning signs.

Warning signs

How can you tell if you're about to make your first mistake in writing risky bail? Look for the warning signs. When bail agents write bonds based on their need for increased cash flow they search for ways to rationalize their decisions. Their thoughts may be something like:

"I really need the money."

"I just need enough money to pay this month's expenses, and then I'll get back on track."

"If I was certain more clients would call, I wouldn't write this bond."

"If the defendant skips, I'll find him."

"The defendant doesn't seem reliable, but the cosigner does."

"I should refer this to another bail agency that's better equipped to handle this risk, but a premium is always better than a referral fee."

"If I don't write some high-risk bail, I'll never get ahead."

"I'll write a risky bond just this once."

Before you make a decision to write bail, ask yourself your reasons for writing this bond. If your reasons are based on sound due diligence, then those are good reasons. However, if you catch yourself rationalizing along the lines of the thoughts we just described, take a moment to stop and reassess the situation.

"I really need the money."

How badly do you really need the money? Will the money make your life significantly better if the bond is risky? How important is the $1,000 premium if it is accompanied by a $10,000 liability headache down the road? If you have to pay the forfeiture on this bond, how much worse will your financial situation become? The need for immediate income is *never* a valid reason for writing a bail bond. Bail agents are in business to write good bonds – to earn steady, reliable income writing bonds for individuals with the greatest likelihood of showing up in court and fulfilling their obligations. Slow and steady is *always* better than risky and inconsistent.

"I just need enough money to pay this month's expenses, and then I'll get back on track."

If this premium helps you catch up this month, what happens next month? And the month after that? If you don't have enough to cover your expenses this month, what makes you think that the situation will improve in the future? If you try to run a bail business without steady cash flow or sufficient operating capital to cover your monthly bills, you are headed for trouble. Writing risky bail will only make the problem worse.

Be very careful not to get into a situation where you can't cover your basic expenses, such as rent and advertising costs, from one month to the next without writing risky bail. This pattern can grow out of control incredibly fast. Faced with bills you can't pay this month, you'll be forced to push them over to the next month to pay them. But next month you'll have a fresh set of bills waiting and you'll have to pay double the usual amount. What will you do then? Write even riskier bail to earn a bigger premium? If you're finding it difficult to cover your basic expenses, you need to stop and rethink your situation. Determine where and how you went off track. Find a way to stabilize your cash flow – without resorting to writing risky bail. There are always positive steps you can take to get your business back on track. Just slow down and focus on steady, reliable growth.

"If I was certain more clients would call, I wouldn't write this bond."

You can never be certain how many clients will call, when, and for how much bail. You will go through dry patches when the phone doesn't ring much – just as you'll experience busy stretches when the phone never seems to stop ringing. You should always have sufficient business reserves to keep your business running during the slow times so that you don't have to resort to writing risky bail just because you need the income from the premiums. If you don't have sufficient reserves, it is time to review your business strategy. Find a way to build up your financial resources without increasing your liability. There is always a way to do this. Take the time to think about it carefully rather than taking the risky shortcut of writing bad bail.

"If the defendant skips, I'll find him."

Can you be certain of that? And do you really want the hassle and expense of tracking him down?

If you hire a bounty hunter, you'll have to pay him a fee (usually between 10-20%) to track down your defendant, in addition to the cost of any phone calls, background searches and other investigative fees. If the bounty hunter locates the defendant out of state you will also have to pay airfare to fly both of them back. Of course you can always search for the defendant yourself. But that will take up valuable time away from the time you could better spend writing bail for reliable people who intend to fulfill their court obligations. You're not a bounty hunter; you're a bail agent. If you're bailing out someone with the assumption that you'll have to track him down, you're not writing bail for the right reasons. Bailing out people that you constantly have to chase is not an effective business strategy. It will not help you grow your business slowly and steadily.

"The defendant doesn't seem reliable, but the cosigner does."

While you want a reliable cosigner, you also want a reliable defendant. You don't want to bail out someone who's going to skip, regardless of how much you trust the cosigner and how carefully you have verified your assumptions with background and collateral checks. Sure, a reliable cosigner means you'll have collateral to cover the forfeiture. But this leads to headaches you don't really want. If the bail amount is low enough, around $20,000, most cosigners won't let their house be foreclosed on. They will find another way to pay the $20,000.

Meanwhile, you will have to pay the $20,000 to the court. Keep in mind that you can only sue the cosigner for the money after you have incurred the loss. If the cosigner doesn't come up with the money, you can foreclose on the property. But that process is a hassle and always entails a degree of uncertainty. You will also have to incur the cost of tracking down the defendant and add that to the list of items the cosigner will need to reimburse. Moreover, your surety company can still drop you, even if you cover the loss. Remember that for the surety company a forfeiture is an indication of risk. The forfeiture is a red flag that suggests that you wrote risky bail.

Another consideration: If you don't trust the defendant, how certain can you be that the cosigner is trustworthy? Even if everything seems to check out, appearances can be deceiving. I've come across cosigners that seemed above board but then later I discovered that they had lied about their information or had deceived me by pulling equity out of their house before I could file my lien on the house.

If you have a bad feeling about a defendant, do not write the bail. Remember that the purpose of the bail system is to guarantee the defendant will *fulfill his obligations* to the court. Every bond you write should be with that purpose in mind.

"I should refer this to another bail agency that's better equipped to handle this risk, but a premium is always better than a referral fee."

If you can develop relationships with other bail agents willing to write riskier bail, you can refer questionable bonds to them. They'll pay you a referral fee which can be anywhere from 10-30% of their premium. This is a good way to earn some cash flow without the liability of writing a bond. Too many agents are reluctant to send referrals to other agencies, because the premium they could earn writing the bond is much higher than the referral fee. The desire to earn a premium instead of a referral fee, however, is not a sound basis for deciding whether or not to write a bond. While a good premium is better than a referral fee, a bad premium never is. If the bond is later forfeited you would have been much better off earning the referral fee.

Too often, bail agents overlook the value of referral fees. If you are networked with a bail company that typically writes higher-risk bail, why not refer higher-risk clients and take the referral fees without the liability? This will give you some cash flow without the risk.

"If I don't write some high-risk bail, I'll never get ahead."

That's simply not true. In fact, the opposite is true: To get ahead, you need to write good, low-risk bail, and do it consistently. That is the best way to ensure a reliable income and steady business growth. Writing high-risk bail only makes you vulnerable to skips, forfeitures and even the loss of your business. Bail agents who focus on writing good bail at a manageable pace are the ones with a thriving business.

"I'll write a risky bond just this once."

This remark should set off some alarm bells. The fact that you're considering a risky bond – even once – means you are likely to do it again. Why? Because you have managed to rationalize the need to write a risky bond, which means that in your mind you now consider it an acceptable risk. Don't fool yourself. If you have found it acceptable once you will find it acceptable again – the next time you are in a similar predicament. By writing a risky bond you also miss the valuable opportunity to reassess your situation. If you are facing difficulties in your business see it as the chance to take positive steps now before things get worse. You can determine why your expenses are too high or why your cash flow is too low. You can find lower-risk ways to improve your business strategy so that you won't face the need to write risky bonds ever again.

How to avoid trouble

With some careful planning and good thinking, you can avoid the trouble of writing bad bail. From the moment you start your business, concentrate on writing bail for people who demonstrate their intention to fulfill all their obligations to the court and deal with cosigners who provide sufficient collateral. Remember that this is the whole purpose of the bail system.

Think of the bail bond you write in terms of the cash value of the bond. If you're handing the defendant $10,000, what are the odds you'll get that money back? Will he show up and fulfill all his obligations to the court? If something goes wrong and the defendant skips, despite your due diligence, have you secured sufficient collateral from the cosigner to cover the loss? In the next chapter, we will discuss the due diligence that will help you answer these questions. Instinct also plays a role. Often you can tell right away that a bond will be too risky to write.

If a corporate vice president who earns $80,000 a month and has lived in the community for the past 40 years calls to bail out his son, a university student with a good record who got into his first bar fight, you probably won't think twice about writing the bail.

If, on the other hand, a guy calls about his buddy who's in jail on dope charges, neither of them works, neither of them owns a car, and the guy offers merely your $1,000 premium plus a pair of Nikes as collateral you are probably making a bad decision to write that bail. The defendant's friend might be a drug dealer who lives out of state. While you'll earn a quick $1,000 writing the bail, you stand to lose $10,000 when the defendant skips and forfeits the bond, and you'll spend $2,000 or more in fees to the bounty hunter you hire to track him. If you decide to track him yourself, you'll be losing valuable hours of your time – hours you could be spending writing good bail and growing your business steadily. Generally speaking, when family calls on behalf of a defendant it is more likely to turn out to be a good bond. When friends call, the opposite is usually true. Defendants are more likely to skip on friends than on family. This doesn't mean that all situations in which a cosigner calls to bail out a family member will be low risk, however, or that a friend calling to bail out a friend will be high risk. It's just a guideline. You still need to base all your final decisions on your background and collateral checks. In other words, you still need to carry out your due diligence.

Conduct an initial risk assessment

Because it takes time for you to run background checks and verify collateral, it's best if you get into the habit of making an initial risk assessment when you first talk to a client over the phone – before you decide to investigate the situation further. As you talk to the client, ask yourself if this is really a situation you want to be involved in. If any alarm bells sound in your head trust your instincts. That is the perfect time to refer the client to another bail agency and collect a referral fee.

As a rule of thumb, if you have to think about a bail situation too long then it probably is not a good bond to write. Rather than fall into a pattern of rationalization, just make a decision to refer the client to another bail agency and collect a referral fee, or decline the case and move on. It's simply not worth the risk of a forfeiture to write a bail bond when you are uncertain. It' is not worth wasting your time to investigate further because you could be missing other clients that call with better bail. This doesn't mean you have to stick to writing "safe" $500 bonds for college students from upstanding families. You can write higher bonds and still minimize your risk of forfeiture through careful research. But do your homework and be as certain as possible that the collateral offered will cover your liability just in case things go wrong.

Aim for slow and steady growth

The best way to avoid writing risky bail is to have no immediate need for large premiums. If you manage your bail business by focusing on slow and steady growth, you won't become desperate for money. If you try to grow too quickly, on the other hand, you might have trouble keeping up with your expenses. You'll be more likely to take the next call that comes in – regardless of how high the risk might be. Be disciplined with your business and you will experience lasting success.

3

COMPLETE YOUR DUE DILIGENCE

The most successful bail agents have built their companies based on careful due diligence. Initial assessments, background checks, verified collateral, completed paperwork – these are your best keys to slow and steady growth. Due diligence will help you avoid forfeitures and protect you in the event that a forfeiture does occur.

It's surprising how often bail agents are tempted to skip steps in their due diligence. Neglecting even one small step can result in forfeitures and insufficient collateral. If a defendant gives you a non-working phone number, for example, and you don't find out until after you receive his forfeiture notice, it will be much harder to locate him. If a cosigner doesn't really possess the title to a property the time to find out is before you write the bond -- not after the defendant skips. You need to perform thorough due diligence on *every* bond you write. Fortunately due diligence is not a difficult or expensive process for the bail agent. It just requires discipline. Let's look at why some bail agents fall short on due diligence and how you can avoid that problem.

Pressures of the industry

Given the importance of due diligence, why do bail agents fail to take important steps? Why do they take shortcuts or offer lenient requirements? Don't they care about their own financial risk? They do care, but the problem lies in the fast pace and competitive nature of the bail industry.

Rushing to be first

Bail agents often feel rushed to write bonds. Defendants do not want to stay in jail a moment longer than they need to. So if you don't move quickly to write a bond, you might lose out to a competitor that responded faster. When you first take a call you often wish you were at the jail already to write the bond because you know that another bondsman might be working on the same bond simultaneously. A cosigner might call you to write the bond, for example, but the defendant is talking meanwhile to a bail agent who happened to be at the jail at the time. You might show up at the jail 20 minutes later with all the paperwork completed only to discover the defendant has already been released under another bail agent's bond. In other cases the defendant has called both a family member and a friend for help and while the family member called you, the friend called another bondsman who showed up at the jail first.

This happened to me recently. A father called me to write a bond for his son who had been arrested and when I arrived at the jail with the father to write the bond, we found that the son was already out. A friend of his had called another bondsman whose office was located closer to the jail. Such is the time pressure bail agents are under every day of their working lives.

Loose requirements

To stay competitive, bail agents are also tempted to offer loose requirements on collateral and premiums. Aware that many incoming calls are potential clients shopping around for the most favorable collateral requirements or payment options, bail agents are often too eager to close the deal and are tempted to offer terms that are too lenient. The danger here is that you will end up with insufficient or no collateral to cover a forfeited bond. If you didn't collect your premium up front you won't even have that as compensation if the defendant and cosigner skip without paying.

Where does the trouble start?

Whenever you rush through the bail bond process, you are asking for trouble. Due diligence requires *time* and effort. It doesn't take that much time to do things right if you make a habit of it; but when you allow yourself to feel the pressure of the industry, spending even a few minutes on due diligence might seem like an eternity. You erroneously have the impression that the due diligence process for the bond you are currently writing is taking time away from writing the next client.

Cutting corners increases risk

When you approach the business with a sense of urgency you are more likely to ignore important steps or make mistakes. If you keep repeating the same mistakes you'll find yourself juggling too many open cases, with too much liability... and with still more bonds coming in. Because you already feel that you're running behind, you'll be tempted to continue to skip due diligence steps. This is a bad pattern to get into, and it is a hard one to break unless you slow your volume and catch up on all your paperwork. Even then it might be too late to obtain some vital information or documents. But by recognizing the pattern and stopping it in its tracks, at least you can avoid making more mistakes. Then you can get caught up and work to minimize the risk you have already undertaken.

Ignoring due diligence means trouble

While you should never cut corners in due diligence, it is even worse to skip due diligence entirely. Too often, bail agents do exactly that. You can avoid this problem by learning to recognize risky situations. Let's say you are tempted to tell a client you'll meet him at the jail right away, post the bond and then complete the paperwork later. Is this a good decision?

Think about this situation: It's after hours. You're busy juggling several bail bonds at once, and you have stacks of bills to pay at the end of the month. A father is calling to bail out his son. The father sounds honest and professional. He says he's the vice president of a major local company, and he's been a resident in the community for the past 50 years. Everything sounds good, and you know that if you don't get to the jail quickly, another agent might write the bond. Because you're in a hurry, you might decide to go straight to the jail, post the bond, and then drive the defendant to his father's house to sign the paperwork. Or you might ask the father to meet you at the jail, but while you're waiting for him to drive the distance, you go ahead and post bail and the defendant is released from custody.

This is a big mistake. You've just let a defendant out of jail without any signed document, without collateral and without having received your premium. What if the defendant runs before his father arrives at the jail? What if you drive the defendant to his father's house and he jumps out while you're stopped at a red light? What if the father refuses to sign the documents or pay your premium, now that his son is out of jail? What if the father isn't who he claimed to be? Even if you caught the defendant, rearrested him and took him back to the jail, you've already posted his bail. You have to get that bond exonerated. This means you must appear in court and explain to the judge why you rearrested the defendant right away. The judge might exonerate the bond without question. Or he might ask you: "Why did you post bail for someone you had to re-arrest immediately and without signed paperwork?" You'll be forced to explain to the judge why you were careless. This is not a comfortable position to be in. You can be certain your surety company won't approve either.

Bailing out a defendant without completing the paperwork is never a good strategy. If you walked into your local bank and asked them for a $10,000 loan without filling out any paperwork or offering any collateral, do you think they'd give you the money? Even if you are creditworthy and have a solid history with them they won't give you the first dollar without going through some type of official process with strict requirements. Why, then, should you write a bond without completing the paperwork, securing collateral and performing due diligence? Even if the defendant seems honest he might be facing jail time he doesn't want to serve. Do your due diligence completely, so you can minimize your risk.

Warning signs

Why do some bail agents cut corners or fail to complete due diligence, when they know it's risky? Sometimes when an agent is swamped with cases, it's difficult to see how many corners are being cut. They do it without thinking through the consequences. They don't take time to focus on whether or not they're doing the job correctly. This is unfortunate, because thorough due diligence doesn't require as much time as they might think.

You can avoid falling into this trap if you become familiar with the warning signs:

1. Incomplete paperwork

As with other legal- and government-related professions, the bail industry requires a large amount of paperwork. For every bond you write you have to file the appropriate papers with the court and the surety company. You need to maintain transaction records and keep files containing documents such as deeds of trust on property, bail agreements, applications, disclosures, receipts, files, etc. In such a paper-driven environment, it's tempting to look for ways to streamline your paperwork. Unfortunately this decision often comes at the expense of due diligence. Look at your defendant and cosigner applications. Are you asking enough questions? Are you rushing through the process and skipping over questions you know are critical?

For each new client, you should ask yourself what is the worst thing that would happen to you if this client forfeited his bond. If the answer is that you would likely end up paying the forfeited bond, because you don't have sufficient information to track him down or sufficient collateral to cover the forfeit – or you're not sure if it's sufficient – then you need to improve your due diligence process.

2. Shortcuts

How many shortcuts have you built into your due diligence procedures? Bail agents who have been in the business a while often rely on their instincts in deciding whether to write a particular bond or require collateral from a particular client. Consciously or not, they rely on shortcuts in due diligence. New agents encounter the same problem when they become too overwhelmed with the volume of work to complete every due diligence step for every bond. The moment you make the decision not to research something completely or to require collateral in a situation of uncertainty, you are placing your business at risk. The defendant might seem sincere and the cosigner might seem reliable. What if they aren't? What if your instincts, that have always been right so far, are wrong just this once? It takes only one bad bond to put you out of business. Would you take the shortcut today if you knew that six months down the road it will come back to haunt you? It's troublesome enough if you take shortcuts on just one potentially bad bond. But when shortcuts become a business standard you need to rethink the way you do business. Ask yourself, *why* you are taking so many shortcuts? Is it because you are writing too many bonds too quickly? Because you have too many phone calls coming in at once?

If you're inundated with new clients and tempted to write bail for every one of them perhaps you have overextended your business or have too much overhead and need to earn as much as possible to cover it. If so, it's time to fix the real problems, get your business back on track and break out of your habit of taking shortcuts in due diligence.

3. Avoid unnecessary liability

Collateral can mean the difference between covering a forfeited bond and going out of business. Unfortunately, the value of any collateral you require is only as good as the due diligence you perform. If you accept collateral but don't research it thoroughly you may find that the collateral is useless when it is already too late to do anything about it.

If a client says he has $100,000 in equity in his house, and you take his word for it, you're going to be in trouble when his $50,000 bond is forfeited and you discover the house only has $25,000 in equity. Instead of reducing your liability, the collateral has become an unnecessary liability – because you failed to perform due diligence. If you don't research the collateral you accept from a client you might as well not ask for any collateral at all. Unfortunately a large number of bail agents don't require collateral on many bonds. They know prospective clients are shopping around to find the easiest collateral requirements. Before you get into a habit of leniency with your collateral requirements, in the belief you will be more competitive, ask yourself how reliable those clients really are. Are you completely certain they will not forfeit their bonds? Are their premiums worth the liabilities you've accepted? If not, you need tougher collateral standards to eliminate unnecessary liability.

4. Too many accounts receivable

Bail agents who want to remain competitive are also tempted to offer payment plans on their premiums. On the larger bonds, $100,000 or more, it's difficult for most clients to come up with the 10% premium payment up front. Unfortunately, every time you agree to accept partial payments for premiums you risk never getting paid at all. Meanwhile you've already written the bond and accepted liability for the full bond amount. It's bad enough if you have to cover a forfeited bond of $100,000 when all you've received for your trouble is a $10,000 premium. But what if all you've received is a partial payment of $3,500, and the client disappears without paying the rest? If you do this too many times, you'll find it impossible to run your business successfully.

If you offer payment plans once in a while, you're probably going to be able to stay on top of the situation – particularly if you've performed thorough due diligence on the client. But if you begin a practice of accepting all premiums on payment plans, you will have too many accounts receivable and thus too much liability.

The situation is worse when you combine payment plans with shortcuts on due diligence. You'll have open accounts receivable files with little information to track down payments. Ironically, if you have any hope of being paid, you've just increased your paperwork tremendously in your effort to track down clients that owe you money. It's better not to have taken the shortcuts or the unnecessary liability in the first place.

How to avoid trouble

The best way to minimize your risk on a new client is to perform the most thorough due diligence. Don't take shortcuts. Don't loosen your requirements just to increase your competitiveness. All it takes is one missing piece of vital information or one missing document to turn a $1,000 premium into a $10,000 headache – the higher the premium, the bigger the headache. Completing your due diligence thoroughly is a very manageable process and a sound business practice. Your due diligence should consist of four major steps:

1. Research your client prior to posting bail.
2. Ask the right questions.
3. Secure the collateral.
4. Collect your premium.

The more you get into the habit of completing these steps, the more successful your business will become.

1. Research your client prior to posting bail.

This doesn't mean you have to research every single client who comes through the door. Some will be obviously above-board, and if the bail amount is small, let's say under $5,000, your liability will be limited. But if you are going to write a large bond, and you want to determine whether or not this defendant is worth the risk of bailing out, it doesn't take much time or cost much to perform a quick background check.

A simple background check

Anybody can perform a background check through the Internet. The cost ranges from $35 to $200. If you have any concerns about the defendant the background check will either turn up information that confirms your concerns or it will reassure you that the case looks good. Either way, the cost of the background check is negligible compared to a $20,000 or even a $100,000 headache. Don't let the availability of information on the Internet fool you into thinking you can easily find a defendant that skips. Many people seem to think – from watching television and movies – that if a person uses a phone in the middle of Manhattan, that person can be pinned down to the street corner he's standing on. Reality is not like that.

You can't depend on being able to find someone that doesn't want to be found. This is where your initial research becomes vital. If you are writing bail for a college student whose parents live in the community and seem to be upstanding citizens with high-level jobs that they have held for years, then the risk is probably low. The defendant is not likely to leave town, and if he does he won't get far because he is probably relying on his parents' bank account. But if the defendant lives alone, with no ties to the community and no regular job, he could easily skip and prove very difficult to find.

Don't depend on bounty hunters for every bond

Some bail agents count on bounty hunters to find everyone that's going to skip town. They figure the premium is worth the risk. If the defendant skips, they'll simply track him down. Unfortunately tracking down a defendant is anything but simple, and it is not cheap either. What happens if the skip goes to Peru or Germany or Korea? You'll have to cover the bounty hunter's travel expenses, in addition to his fee. Relying on a bounty hunter is not a good business model for a successful bail agent. It's not a reliable way to make decisions on whether or not to bail out a defendant. Bounty hunters should be treated as a resource only when everything else has failed.

People do forfeit bonds, and you might encounter a situation in which you thought a defendant was reliable, backed up by your due diligence, yet he skipped anyway. In that situation, you will most likely call a bounty hunter and try to find the defendant. This should happen rarely, however, and it should never be a consideration in determining whether or not to write a bond. If you feel uncertain about a defendant but you agree to write the bail anyway with the thought that you can always call a bounty hunter, you are exposing yourself to failure—you've written a bad bond.

If you have to debate, say "No"

A good rule of thumb is that if you have to spend more than 5 to 10 minutes debating whether or not you should bail out someone, the answer is either "No" or "Require more collateral." If you can't make a quick decision you're probably moving into something beyond your comfort level of risk. There's a reason why you start to think, "If he skips, where am I going to have to chase him?" Your instincts are telling you that it is probably not the best bond for you to write.

This is where referral fees become important. If you were going to write a $50,000 bond, earn $5,000 but take on $50,000 of liability – particularly for a defendant that raised too many questions in your mind – now you can refer the bond to someone else, earn a $1,000 referral fee, have zero liability and sleep well at night.

2. How to ask effective questions.

Your due diligence is only as effective as the questions you ask new clients – defendants and cosigners. *(For a sample new client questionnaire, see Appendix.)* Following are a few typical questions to ask:

1. Where do the defendant and cosigner live, and how long have they lived there? Where do most of their family members live?
2. Where are the defendant and cosigner employed? How long have they worked for their current employer and/or in their current industry?
3. Do the defendant and cosigner live in a house or an apartment, and how long have they lived there?
4. What are the defendant's and cosigner's personal assets?
5. Do the defendant and cosigner have any past criminal records, and if so, what are the details?
6. What is the situation or story behind the defendant's arrest?

Ask open-ended questions

When you're first evaluating a client, it's important that you ask *open-ended* questions. These are the questions that require more than a simple "Yes" or "No" answer. If you ask, "Do you work?" and the answer is "Yes," that doesn't tell you much. It is a closed question. If you ask instead, "What kind of work do you do?" you might discover that the client doesn't have a reliable job. Without asking the client to think about his answers and elaborate on everything you might have a client that looks good on paper but is, in reality, a risk. For example, if this is the defendant's "third strike" and he will be convicted this time, that's valuable information you need to know up front – and you won't get this information without asking.

When deciding whether or not to write a particular bond, a valid question to ask the cosigner is, "If the defendant were to skip town, how would you pay off the bond?" This is a good way to get an extra read on the person. He might be prepared to lie about other information, e.g., his phone numbers, where he works or where his family lives, but he won't necessarily lie about how he would pay off the bond. The question is unexpected and forces the cosigner to think. It gives him a sense of reality and allows you to determine whether or not the cosigner seems like a responsible person. You'll know by his answer whether or not he is likely to look for all possible avenues to pay off the bond in the event the defendant skips. If the cosigner offers his home as collateral, it is also important to ask the right questions about the property: How much equity does he have in the home, and what is the approximate value of the home? Regardless of whether or not his answers seem valid, it is important to follow up collateral offers with solid research.

3. Secure collateral.

Before accepting collateral on a bond you need to ensure that the client actually owns the property and that the equity value of the property is what he claims it to be - or how close to the amount he claims.

Automobiles as collateral

To look up the market value of an automobile you can consult the Kelly Blue Book online at http://www.kbb.com. While the Kelly Blue Book is a good guide to the current value of the car, you might want to subtract somewhat from that amount as the actual value that you would get will probably be less. With this information, you can determine whether or not the car provides sufficient collateral to make the bond a good risk. Then you need to decide whether you want to hold the car in your possession or just hold the title. Some bail agents don't want the hassle of collecting and holding the car considering the storage fees they might have to pay. But you need to make our own assessment of whoever is offering the car as collateral. Do you trust them not to skip town in the car, hide it or sell it and then claim that they lost the title? If you decide that it is an acceptable risk to just hold the title do you want to hold it in the client's name or perfect the title in your name? If you leave the title in the client's name, the client can go to the DMV claiming that they lost the title and have a new one issued. This is a fraudulent act, but whether or not someone is willing to commit fraud depends on the person and the situation.

Everything comes down to the due diligence you perform on the client. If the client checks out as a responsible person who will likely value his car more than the collateral amount it might be an acceptable risk to hold onto the title in his name. If not, you might be accepting unnecessary liability by not perfecting the title in your name or taking possession of the vehicle.

Homes as collateral

For a house, your research might include driving by the house to see if a client's alleged million-dollar home is really located in a million-dollar neighborhood and to be sure that the house hasn't caught fire, been condemned, or put up for sale – if a client is trying to use a property as collateral and didn't tell you the house is for sale, the person might be lying or you might eventually run into a problem with ownership. It's always important to confirm the value of the equity in a home offered as collateral. Even if a client is not deliberately trying to deceive you he might have an over inflated opinion of what his house is worth. To determine the true equity you need to look at sales comps for the area to see how much you could sell the house at today's values should you happen to get stuck with it. In addition, you need to know how much the client owes on the mortgage before the house can be paid off.

The amount of the bond also determines whether or not the property is acceptable as collateral. If the bond amount is $10,000, a cosigner probably will not want to lose his home over that amount and will find another way to pay off the forfeited bond if the defendant skips. But if the bond is $100,000 he might be willing to let you take the house especially if he doesn't have close to that amount of equity in it. While this doesn't happen often you can begin to see how the risk of being stuck with collateral – particularly useless collateral – highlights the importance of performing your due diligence upfront.

Title searches are important

Your research on a property might include a title search - particularly important on large bail bonds. You can run a title search through a service such as Dataquick.com, which costs $2 to $5 per search to confirm ownership. This information is necessary to file a deed of trust on the property and might be adequate for smaller bonds. Ownership can be more complicated, however, and it's often better to spend $200 to run a full title report through the county clerk's office – particularly on a large bond for which the amount of liability outweighs the cost of the title report. A full title report will tell you who is on title, how many liens are against the house (and for how much) whether or not the taxes are current, and whether the house has the amount of equity the client claims. It's important to confirm not only that the client owns the house but also how many other people might hold title to the same property. If a client tells you he has $200,000 equity on a home he owns free and clear but neglects to tell you that another person also holds title to the house take that as a good indication you can't trust the person. If the client offers his $1 million-dollar home as collateral and says he has $500,000 in equity, but he neglects to tell you that in addition to several mortgages he has three independent loans on the property totaling $200,000, he is being less than honest and is jeopardizing your claim on the property in the event of a forfeiture.

Unfortunately, if you don't run a full title search, you'll never know that someone else owns a client's property or that the property has other liens against it. Dataquick.com will not provide this depth of information. Even if a client is up-front about shared ownership of a home, you might still face problems accepting the home as collateral. If a property is owned jointly by four family members and the defendant's mother wants to bail him out while her husband is at work, and her brother and sister-in-law live overseas, you might be tempted to accept the collateral based on the mother's signature. This is not a good way to do business. For the document to be fully binding, everyone who holds title to the property should be present to cosign. Otherwise, what happens if the mother dies and her son skips bail? You'll be fighting the other family members for the property. If you're really secure in the bond, and you're not worried the defendant will skip, you might be willing to accept the signatures of the other parties via fax while you write the bond. But you still need to follow up by obtaining the original signatures. Accepting signatures via fax should be the exception rather than the rule. It's not a good habit to get into. In most cases it simply won't be worth the risk.

Collateral with no equity

Not only can a full title report save you from liability in multiple ownership cases, but it can also reveal situations where the equity is not what the client claims it to be. I had clients come in one time for a $100,000 bond. I researched their background and everything checked out all right. By all appearances, they were honest people and an acceptable risk – respectable parents bailing out their son. I did a title search on Dataquick.com and determined they had sufficient equity in their house to accept the property as collateral. Overall I had a good feeling about the situation so I decided to write the bail. A few days later I filed my lien against the property just in case the defendant decided to skip. Six months passed and one day I received notification that the defendant did not appear for his court sentencing. The bond was in forfeit so now I risked losing $100,000 if I didn't locate the defendant. I would have to foreclose on the home instead. Imagine my surprise when, as a lien holder, I received a foreclosure notice on the property – only to discover I was fifth in line. The property had four other loans ahead of me. Their loans would have to be settled by proceeds from the foreclosure sale, ahead of my lien, so there was little chance I would see any money from the sale. How did this happen? Apparently the same day they approached me to write bail, the defendant's parents contacted several loan doctors and drew out all their equity on the property in cash. They did this before I filed my lien. By the time I discovered all this, six months had passed and the defendant was long gone. I had to pay the forfeited bond. Because I didn't have the full amount in my BUF account I had to make payments to the surety company for an entire year. What could I have done differently?

I didn't have to wait several days to file my lien. I could have filed it the same day. This would have increased the likelihood that my lien would be recorded prior to any other loans the defendant's parents took out that day. What if they took out the loans before they came to see me? What could I have done then? I could have done more research prior to posting bail. I could have run a full title report for $200. If I had, I would have discovered the loan doctor activity and would have refused to write bail for the defendant. I should have weighed the $200 title report fee against the $100,000 liability. After all, my premium was $10,000 on this bond. It was worth spending $200 of that premium for added assurance. Even if I had written the bond first and wasn't able to file my lien right away, I still should have run the title report. If I had run the title report a week or two later, I would have realized the equity in the house was gone and I would have had a much easier time finding and re-arresting the defendant. When a court appearance is six months away there's less chance a defendant will skip immediately. It is more likely that he will skip closer to the court date. Thus, having the title report even a few weeks after I wrote the bond would have made a big difference in my liability. This raises the importance not only of performing due diligence *before* you write the bond but also *following up* with additional due diligence. You need to conduct background searches, run title reports and collect as much information as possible ahead of time. But there is also no harm in repeating the process two weeks later, just to be sure everything still looks good. That way, if you discover a problem, you are in a much better position to act than you would be six months down the road when the defendant has already left town.

4. Collect your premium.

Your premium is how you earn your living as a bail agent. Unfortunately, in the bail industry we often deal with individuals who wouldn't think twice about paying our premiums with bounced checks or stolen credit cards. Due diligence can prevent a client from cheating you out of your premium. Because the cosigner is usually the person paying the premium – as well as offering the collateral – you need to get to know the cosigner extremely well. You need to research just as much background information on the cosigner as you do on the defendant.

Don't assume family is reliable
I mentioned that family members are often more reliable as cosigners than friends. This doesn't mean individuals bailing out family members are always honest. Long ago, I received a call from a woman wanting to bail out her husband. He was arrested for writing bad checks which should have set off alarm bells.

They seemed like nice, decent, trustworthy people. I assumed the defendant was either innocent or had just used poor judgment on this one occasion. Besides, the wife offered to pay my premium by signing over a check she had coming in from a major insurance company. The amount of the check was enough to cover my premium. She told me she'd sign the check over to me, and I could refund her the difference. Because the check was from a major insurance company, I knew I didn't have to worry about fraud—it wasn't as if the defendant was writing me a bad check. I deposited the check into my bank – a large national bank – and they accepted the check with no problem. I bailed out the defendant. Within a week, he was back in jail, having violated his probation, and a new bail amount was set.

The defendant's wife told me she had received another check for an insurance settlement and would write me a check for my premium against that settlement. Because her previous check from the insurance company had gone through my bank with no problem, I accepted her check. Two weeks after I wrote the first bond, I looked at my bank account statement online and wondered why my balance was short. I called the bank and they told me I had deposited two bad checks, including a fraudulent check from a major insurance company. Finally the police called to tell me the defendant was fraudulently printing the insurance company checks. My national bank didn't even catch the error for two weeks. Fortunately by that time, the defendant was back in jail, having violated his probation again. If they hadn't grabbed him so quickly, not only would I have had nothing to show for my time and effort on the case, but I also would have been left with a huge liability. The defendant was required to pay restitution to me and everyone else he had defrauded. I received a small payment every month.

I learned later that checks have watermarks, and I could have used that to verify the validity of the check. I also could have required payment in cash. Many old-school bondsmen require cash for everything. They have never accepted credit cards or checks and never will, perhaps with good reason – even though it's easier now to accept credit cards and ATM cards with instant verification of funds.

Whatever methods of payment you accept, it's important not to assume someone is honest because they sound trustworthy over the phone. If you do, and they defraud you, they've not only cheated you out of your earnings, but out of the time, money and labor you put into their case.

Keep up with payment plans

If you agree to accept payment plans for premiums, due diligence is also critical. First, you need to determine if the client is trustworthy enough to pay in installments. In addition, you need to be prepared to follow up actively to ensure all payments are made. If you have too many outstanding accounts receivable it will be hard for you to keep track. The longer you wait to follow up on a missing payment, the harder it might be to locate the client or force him to pay. This is not an effective way to approach the business. If you're not receiving full premiums, you aren't being rewarded for your work and you are possibly not receiving enough to cover your expenses for writing the bond. Regardless of how much the client pays you up front, you still have to pay your bond cost to the surety, which can be anywhere from 10-25% of the premium amount, along with a 10% deposit into your BUF account. For example, if a client owes you a $1,000 premium on a $10,000 bond, and you ask the client to put $300 down, you'll be required to deposit 10% or $100 into your BUF account, and your bond cost will be anywhere from $100 to $500. That means you have earned $300 but paid out $200 to $600. You've netted nothing for your time and effort, perhaps paid out more than you've earned and you have an account receivable that you'll need to spend more time and effort following up. If the client doesn't pay what he owes, you'll either need to turn it over to a collections agency for a 40% fee or go after the client yourself, taking your time away from marketing your business or writing more bail. In other words you'll be using good money to chase bad money. Moreover, your liability remains the same, yet you've earned less money to compensate for a forfeited bond. Remember the rule of thumb that it takes 18 bonds of equal size to pay off one forfeited bond. If you've accepted only $1,500 down on a $5,000 premium now you need to increase the number of bonds you will write if the defendant forfeits on the $50,000 bond and fails to pay the balance due on your premium.

This doesn't mean it's a bad idea to accept payment plans. Just be sure you're doing it for the right reasons, i.e., to help somebody out or to benefit your company, rather than out of desperation to write the next bond that comes along so you can get out of a financial hole. Always keep in mind that payment plans increase your liability and risk. It's all right to offer them when your business is up and everything is going well. But if your business is down accepting partial payments causes you to lose your edge even further making you even more desperate to write the next bond. Once again, in all of these matters, the simple but effective key to avoiding trouble is due diligence. Put due diligence procedures into place, keep checking yourself to be sure you're following them carefully, and you will avoid the problems that cause other bail businesses to fail. Due diligence is your key to achieve lasting success.

4

GROWING STEADILY

When you're starting a new bail bond business, it's easy to feel overwhelmed by all the competition and all the avenues for advertising. Many new bail agents decide that in order to get their new business off the ground and to be competitive, they need high visibility in terms of advertising and physical location. The temptation can be great to take out yellow page ads in as many phone books as possible, to take out billboard ads on the freeway and bus bench ads near the courthouse, and to set up an office right across the street from the jail – an office that remains open 24 hours a day, seven days a week. While these are all good routes to potential success for your bail bond company, it's easy to take on too much too quickly. If the yellow page advertisements prove successful, the phone will begin to ring incessantly. The volume of incoming calls will appear to validate the measures you have taken to gain exposure. The prospect of writing as much bail as possible, as quickly as possible, will become very attractive – a sign of your success.

Because a fast-growing business feels successful, it's hard to recognize the danger until it's almost too late. By the time you realize what's happening, your overhead advertising costs are enormous and you feel forced to write riskier bail just to cover your monthly bills. You are caught in the vicious circle of writing bail just to earn the premiums – and setting yourself up for huge liability down the road all because you took out too many advertisements and tried to grow too quickly.

Let's look at a common problem among new bail agents: taking out too many yellow page ads. Then we will discuss how you can avoid this problem by growing your business slowly and steadily.

Working for the phone company

When you open a new bail agency, it's tempting to take out as many yellow page ads as possible. It seems a relatively small investment for a great amount of exposure. But if you're not careful, the costs and obligations can catch up with you, and before you realize what's happening, you're practically working for the phone company. How does this happen?

Many yellow page books

There's not just one yellow page phone book in your area. Depending on where you live, there may be a dozen from one company and a dozen from another. Your first ad will likely be in the most prominent yellow pages book, e.g., Verizon, SBC, etc. Then you'll discover a local book that is so inexpensive compared to the others – perhaps you can place an ad in that book for $300 per month. You know that all you need is one $3,000 bond per month to cover the cost of that ad, so it seems like a good deal. But what happens when you apply that logic to dozens of other phone books? Or when you decide to increase your quarter-page ad to a full-page ad, so you can have double the business exposure? The cost might increase by $100 per ad, which seems reasonable, until you multiply it by the number of phone books in which you have taken out ads. Suddenly your monthly advertising bill is astronomical. You might not notice the expense at first, particularly if you're writing a $15,000 bond each month from incoming calls based on each phone book ad. But then one month you might not receive any calls from several of the books. When this lull occurs, the phone book ads stop paying for themselves. What then? Do you wait and give them another month? What if they still don't pull any new calls? Now you're depending on the other phone books to pay not only for themselves, but also for the phone books that aren't pulling new calls.

Thus begins a juggling game with phone book ads. It's an expensive game, one that tempts you to write riskier bail so you earn enough premiums to pay your monthly expenses for the phone book ads. This is not a good business plan. You might as well be on the payroll of the phone company.

A silent partner with no liability

Even if you can cover all the costs of your yellow page book ads, if you're paying the phone company $10,000 per month and you earn $20,000 per month, the phone company is now an equal and silent partner in your business. The phone company is a partner only in terms of profit, however, because they carry none of your liability. If your business goes down, you as the owner will take the hit, but the phone company will continue to receive their monthly advertising fees from you. They're not paying your forfeitures or your bond costs to the surety company or the mortgage or rental fees on your office space.

And they are the ones to have their hand in the pot first when you get paid.

When I first started out, I was paying $20,000 a month in phone book advertising. I typically earned $50,000 a month, but not all of that was from phone book ads. Some of my income was from repeat clients and attorney referrals. Moreover, I had to use part of my income to pay for my other overhead costs, in addition to my phone book advertising. But the phone company always received my $20,000 each month. They were a silent partner that carried none of my liability.

Each ad should cover three times its cost

While most ads pay for themselves in terms of the new business they generate, it's not worth the risk of multiplying your advertising costs by so many phone books and so many ads. If you do, that means every ad must pay for itself every month, with no exceptions. As a rule, each ad should bring you three to five times its cost in terms of new business revenue generated. Unfortunately, there will always be slow months. If you have a slow month, you'll be tempted to place some of your phone book advertising bills on the back burner, assuming the next month will be better and you'll be able to cover them. What happens if the situation next month isn't better? What if you have to pay a forfeiture? Suddenly you have double the advertising bills and double the stress. The next $100,000 bond that comes in the door is going to look very tempting, regardless of whether or not it's a good risk. When your phone book advertising costs make you desperate, you start to gamble on which bonds to write. Your standards go down because you make decisions you wouldn't have made if you weren't desperate to pay your bills. Fear creeps in and you start to rationalize writing bonds that you shouldn't be touching. The best way to avoid this trouble is by understanding where it starts. There is a fine balance between using yellow page ads to grow your business and getting carried away with too many ads.

As long as you can learn to recognize how many ads are sufficient, and when you need to drop an ad that's not carrying its weight, you can manage your advertising effectively. Yellow page ads are the number one source of new business for bail agents. You just need to use this source wisely. So let's look at where the trouble starts so you can avoid it.

Where does the trouble start?

It seems logical to start a new business slowly, limiting your advertising to what you can afford, and expanding it as your business grows. Unfortunately, too many new bail agents become ambitious and want faster growth. Others lack confidence in their business strategy and attempt to cover all bases by advertising everywhere. Neither of these is a sound growth strategy. To avoid trouble, you need a solid plan for growing your business through advertising.

Don't try to corner the market

As a new bail agent, what are your business goals? Do you have to be the biggest, fastest-growing bail bond business in your region? Do you have to invest in big office space and big advertising in order to go after the most lucrative premiums?

Too many new agents make this decision right from the start. Some take it a step further. They want to become the go-to agency and corner the market. They launch a huge campaign up-front and try to gain exposure everywhere they can. They hope their larger-than-life appearance and sudden notoriety will result in lots of referrals. They want to dominate the industry.

This approach is a gamble in any business endeavor, and it's very hard to maintain in the bail industry. Most of the bail bond companies that try to become superpowers go out of business within a few years, when all their expenses and liabilities catch up to them. Sadly, their surety companies take a hit as well. Depending on the size and stability of the surety company, they might find themselves out of business along with the over-inflated bail agency.

Keep your ambition in check… and trust your plan

While it's great to be eager and enthusiastic when you're first starting out, be sure to keep your ambition in check. Ambition might lead you to overspend on office space, personnel and advertising – too much, too quickly. You will then be tempted to write bail simply for the premiums, to cover your ambitious overhead costs. You won't consider the risk involved in each bond you write.

You don't have to believe you're going to dominate the industry to get into trouble, either. Ambition can be subtle and can sneak up on you when you least expect it. Say that you start out with what you believe is a reasonable advertising budget of $5,000 per month. Business starts to roll in at a fast pace, and while you hadn't intended to be overly ambitious, your quick success lures you into more advertisements or a bigger office space. Suddenly you're in over your head, and when you experience your first slow month, you'll be desperate to write bail for the wrong reasons. Fear is another reason many bail agents grow their business too quickly. Fear that you won't earn enough to stay in business or that you won't earn enough to cover your overhead costs, even if those costs start out low, can drive you to write every bond that comes in the door. This fear can also drive you to expand your advertising costs to bring in more business "just in case" – creating a self-fulfilling prophecy when you truly aren't earning enough to cover those costs.

Warning signs

When bail agents constantly make bad decisions it is often an indicator that they were trying to grow their business too quickly. Or their business might be out of control already and they need to scale back. If they reach this point, it's because they missed some important warning signs. Learn to recognize these signs, and you'll experience greater success with your bail business.

If you catch yourself making a hasty decision, stop and ask yourself whether you are making that decision because you feel pressured by your overhead expenses or by your high volume of incoming calls. If you are making decisions for the wrong reasons, take a step back. Slow down. Rethink your business strategy. This will help you avoid trouble down the road.

Remember the rationalization: "Just let me write these next few risky bonds to get back on track, and then I'll reassess everything." If that thought enters your mind, dismiss it immediately. This will just lead to more rationalization and greater problems. Instead, figure out where you went off track and find a solid way to get yourself back on track.

How to avoid trouble

If you start out with the right approach to your bail business and keep following that strategy carefully, you will avoid the need to make difficult decisions down the road. You should have clear business goals from the very start. Commit to slow, steady and manageable growth. Create a reasonable advertising budget. Take full advantage of attorney referral networks – attorneys will help you bring in more business without huge advertising costs.

Be realistic about the operating capital you need to back up your business strategy. When you start any new business, you should have six months of operating capital set aside to cover your expenses during slow months. If you don't, you should try to accumulate that amount as soon as possible – without resorting to writing risky bail. Get your feet wet and start bringing in some capital by writing a few good bonds here and there. This will allow you to learn the business while maintaining slow and steady growth. You'll avoid being tied into too much overhead and liability. Start out writing smaller, safer bonds until you feel secure moving into something bigger.

With smaller bonds, you won't feel so pressured to offer payment plans to clients, as your premiums per bond will be smaller and more affordable to them. For riskier bonds, set up a referral network with an agency capable of handling the higher risk, and put the referral fees you earn toward your operating capital. Limit your advertising budget to $1,000 a month or less, and think creatively about marketing. If you spend $500 per month on phone book ads, for example, and $500 on advertising to criminal attorneys, the phone books will net you a few calls, but the attorneys will be able to send you business continually.

If the attorneys like the job you're doing they will send you more and more clients, and you won't have to spend much more to advertise to them.

If, on the other hand, you jump into phone book advertising at $10,000 per month without the capital to back it up, you'll end up in trouble. *(For a discussion on planning your phone book advertising, see Chapter 7.)*

Finally, be sure you're not starting a bail agency because you think it's the best way to become rich overnight. No doubt you've seen plenty of so-called "get rich quick" schemes that promise you $1 million by the end of the year. In reality, success rarely happens overnight. Sure, if you follow some "get rich quick" plans, you might earn $1 million in the long run, but it will require closer to five years, not one. It's the same with running a bail bond business. You won't become rich overnight – and if you do, the risks you'll have to take will outweigh the rewards significantly.

But if you focus on steadily growing your business over time it will become a lucrative and stable venture. You'll experience reliable profitability rather than unnecessary liability.

5

PROCESSING PAPERWORK

The bail bond business is driven by information and documentation. Your success as a bail agent depends to a large degree on your ability to manage paperwork and on your ability to follow up on important files. If you let paperwork slide or you let work pile up, you will run into problems.

When you open a new client file, that file remains open until the defendant's court case is resolved. That can take months and sometimes years. Meanwhile, the defendant is out on bail and, if you don't keep track of him, six months down the road he might fail to show up in court. Suddenly you're stuck with a forfeit and unless you can locate the defendant you will have to pay the full amount of the bond. If the defendant does fulfill his obligations to the court, you will be required to return whatever collateral he or his cosigner gave you. If you haven't stayed on top of your paperwork, how easily will you be able to find that collateral and return it? For a bail agent, staying on top of files is not just a matter of efficiency or keeping your office clean. In many instances, it's a requirement of the business. In all instances, it's a practice that can save your business from disaster.

The danger of falling through the cracks

In many businesses, paperwork takes a back seat to all other matters. Because file folders don't call you on the phone and documents don't knock on your door, asking for attention, they are easily ignored. How many offices have you visited, particularly small businesses, where paperwork and file folders are piled up on desks? That doesn't include what you don't see, stuffed away, unorganized, in file cabinets and boxes.

When any small business allows paperwork to pile up and file folders to fall through the cracks, sometimes literally, the risk is high that something important will be overlooked: a bill that wasn't paid, an account receivable that's outstanding, physical proof of a transaction or a document that needs to be returned to its owner. In the bail business, because so many documents and files are connected with high liability risk, the danger in letting work pile up is even greater. If you don't have an organized filing system, a process of completing all paperwork in a timely manner and a strict set of follow-up procedures, you might encounter one or more of the following problems:

1. You might be unaware of a forfeiture notice that was mailed to you three months before you discovered it.

If you don't keep your files organized and stay on top of all cases in which you're involved, you might not be aware of a forfeiture. Courts usually send forfeiture notices to bail agents within 30 days after a defendant fails to appear in court. But it's not a good practice to rely on these court notices to keep tabs on your defendants.

If the court fails to notify you or the notification is lost in the mail or ends up unopened at the bottom of a pile on your desk, several months might go by before you find the notice or the surety company brings the forfeiture to your attention. By then, the defendant will have disappeared, his trail might be cold, and you will have lost your best opportunity to find him. You'll have to pay the forfeiture and absorb the resulting financial impact.

2. You might lack evidence that you performed due diligence on a forfeited bond and wrote what you believed was good bail.

When bail agents write bad bail, surety companies can give them a hard time or at least keep tabs on them. Surety companies are reluctant to provide backing to bail agents that put them unnecessarily at risk. If you have a forfeited bond and the surety company suspects you didn't perform the appropriate due diligence, the company might drop you from its list of agents. You'll be forced to find another surety company to back you and, if you go through this process too many times, you may find yourself out of business.

Sometimes despite your best efforts at due diligence, forfeitures do occur. When this happens, the best you can hope for is that you have secured enough collateral to cover the forfeited bond, and that you've gathered enough information on the defendant for a bounty hunter to find him. But what if you've lost your paperwork or failed to document the due diligence steps you took? Will your surety company believe that you wrote what you believed was good bail with low risk? Will you be able to locate the information the bounty hunter needs to find your defendant? Will you be able to locate the documents that prove the cosigner gave you his collateral?

If you are not organized with your paperwork, you might as well not have performed due diligence or secured collateral in the first place. If you can't locate critical information or documents when you need them, they will do you no good.

3. You might be unable to return collateral when required.

When a bond is forfeited, you need the appropriate documentation to prove you have the collateral to cover it. Likewise, when a defendant fulfills his obligations to the court, you need to return the collateral he or his cosigner gave you.

If you are disorganized or haven't kept your files up to date, you might not know what the defendant or cosigner used for collateral. You might not be able to locate quickly the documents you need to return. Saying, "I know they're here in my office somewhere" is not going to impress a cosigner eager to get his property back. Not to mention that you'll have to put your business on hold temporarily while you search for the missing documents. Moreover, in most states you are legally required to return collateral within 30 days after the bond is exonerated – at which time whoever deposited the collateral with you needs to come in, retrieve it and sign for it. Even if you have secured the collateral documents in a file, and you know how to locate that file, you should also have immediate and easy access to a computer record of what every client has given you by way of collateral in case you need to make a quick decision.

4. You might not receive full payment of your premiums.

Just as it's easy to lose track of who gave you what collateral and when, it's easy to forget who has paid you and how much they have paid to date. Suppose a client handed you $500 in cash for your premium. You deposited it in your business bank account but you forgot to make a note of the transaction in your accounting records and in the client's file. Now you don't remember how much they paid or even if they paid. If the $500 was part of a payment plan but you didn't record the transaction or your payment terms, how will you be able to collect any money they might owe you? Where is your proof that they didn't pay you? You might think you will remember these payment details, but a month or two down the road – and many clients later – you may not. Rather than risk losing track of details, you need to maintain complete and timely records. Keep track of every dime going into and out of your business. It might be wise to hire an accountant to help you with this.

5. You might pay too much or too little on your taxes.

When you run your own bail bond company, you will be responsible for paying taxes on your business earnings. It's important that you keep track of all your receipts for business-related expenditures, so you can claim the appropriate deductions – and it's a good idea to consult with an accountant as to what types of expenses are tax-deductible. If you aren't organized with your transaction records and receipts, when it comes time to pay your taxes, you won't remember how much you spent on what. You'll be forced to estimate your expenses, which means you're likely to claim the wrong amount in deductions. If you claim too much and you're audited, you won't be able to back up your claim with the appropriate records and receipts. You might face steep penalties. If, on the other hand, you claim too little, you'll be paying out more in taxes than you need to. Neither approach is good for you or your business. Thus, it's important to keep current and accurate transaction records and save and organize all your receipts.

Where does the trouble start?

When a bail agent has work piled up everywhere, it indicates the agent is not taking care of administrative tasks on a regular basis. The agent is either disorganized or overwhelmed. Without a good filing and follow-up system in place, and without sufficient time to process paperwork, it's difficult to manage a successful bail bond company. This is not a difficult problem to solve. You just need to make an effort to complete all your paperwork and filing in a timely manner. And you need to allow sufficient time to follow up on all your open cases.

Managing calls and files

Unfortunately, the fast pace of the bail industry distracts many agents from maintaining organized files. Because calls can come in 24 hours a day, seven days a week, you might be busy writing bail and going back and forth to the jail for hours on end for several days in a row. How can you find time to keep up with your administrative tasks, not to mention keeping track of your defendants out on bail?

During a busy stretch, at minimum you need to complete all your paperwork – remember the importance of completing thorough due diligence for every bond you write. If you don't have time to file all your documents, you have two options: wait until the flurry of calls subsides and then be sure to catch up quickly on filing or hire temporary or permanent office assistance to help you keep up with the organizational workload.

Organization is not a luxury

Too many new bail agents don't consider their administrative work to be as important as generating new business and revenue. They either spend all their downtime networking and looking for more ways to advertise, or resting and recovering so they can dive back in and write more bail. Some are so busy trying to find new clients that they consider downtime a luxury they can't afford. They consider administrative tasks and organization to be a luxury as well – something they'll worry about after they've established their business and have sufficient cash flow to hire an office assistant. After all, who really needs a clean desk? A busy-looking office is a sign that business is good, right?

Administrative tasks and an organized office might seem like a luxury at first, or a waste of time. When you're filing documents, completing paperwork, calling the courts to be sure that your defendants have shown up, or calling clients to follow up on accounts receivable, you're not doing what you consider most important: writing bail, bringing in new clients, generating revenue. The caveat is that if you don't complete administrative tasks thoroughly and in a timely manner, you risk falling into liability that will hurt your business. The problem becomes magnified when a new bail agent has grand ideas about how big his business will become and how much he profit he will earn. If his goals are too ambitious, how can he possibly take time out to stay organized?

It's often not until trouble arises that bail agents recognize the importance of maintaining complete and organized files, and by then it may be too late. When they are facing a forfeiture, required to return collateral or desperate for money they could have earned by staying on top of accounts receivable, suddenly administrative tasks are no longer seen as a luxury. The agent is now in a difficult position that might have been avoided if only he had paid attention to the warning signs.

Warning signs

Perhaps the only benefit to letting work literally pile up is that you have a very visible, physical indication that you're falling behind. If you have stacks of file folders on your desk or documents piled high in a "to be filed" basket, it will be very easy to see that you are headed for trouble. There is a different kind of disorganization that is more difficult to spot. It happens when you file away incomplete documents or close accounts prematurely, or when you stuff bundles of miscellaneous papers into boxes and hide them in a storage closet to keep your office space clean. Out of sight might be out of mind, but that doesn't mean it should be. If you find it overwhelming or difficult to locate information in your files, or if you find yourself setting paperwork aside to complete later – then never returning to it – there's a good chance that you are letting work pile up. You need to make time to catch up, and then set new systems and procedures into place before your lack of organization creates big trouble. Are you falling behind in your administrative tasks? See if you can pass this organizational test:

1. If you needed to prove you hold title to a client's property, could you locate that proof quickly?

2. Could you determine quickly which defendants you have out on bail?

3. Do you know if all your accounts receivable are up to date?

4. Do you have a specific procedure in place for opening and following up on new client files?

5. If someone were to audit all your client files, would you feel confident they'd find all your paperwork complete?

6. If a defendant called to ask when and where he's supposed to appear in court, could you find the information while he's still on the line?

7. If a defendant's bail were exonerated, would you know what collateral you would need to return, if any, and would you have the appropriate documents readily available?

8. Are you confident that every one of your defendants out on bail is current on his court appearances?

9. If you were given one day to prepare all records and receipts for your tax returns, would you be able to produce an accurate itemization of deductions?

10. Do you know whether or not you've reached a point where you need to hire an office assistant?

If you were able to answer "Yes" to every one of these questions, you're well on your way to running an organized bail bond business. If not, you know where to focus your efforts.

How to avoid trouble

The best way to avoid trouble with paperwork and administrative tasks is to put good organizational systems into place from the moment you start your business. You should have systems in place for every job function and every task. The better your filing and follow-up procedures are, the more successful your bail bond business will be. Following are some guidelines for getting organized:

1. Set up a good filing system.

Organization begins with a good filing system. For each client, you'll need to keep specific documents on hand. The most important documents are your copy of the bail bond, the bail agreement and the applications, but you will also need to keep any plain-talk contracts or other forms the cosigner filled out. You might also have notes you jotted down during your various phone conversations with the cosigner or defendant. If collateral is involved, you'll also need to file documents such as the deed of trust, lien paperwork, vehicle title and collateral receipts.

I create a manila folder for each client and keep all related documents in the folder. Other bail agents staple documents together or use hole punchers to keep everything in binders or file folders with fasteners. It doesn't matter how you choose to store the documents, as long as all information and paperwork pertaining to a particular client is kept organized and in one location that's easy to find.

It's often helpful to assign a file number to each case to allow you to reference it quickly – this is particularly important if you have a computerized system.

If you have a good filing system, you'll know what to do with every document that crosses your desk. If you have a document pertaining to a client's payment plan, you will know to put that document in your designated collections file cabinet or desk. If you have a document for which you need more information from the defendant to complete, you will know to put that document in your "Needs More Info" basket. You'll also have a place to put forfeiture notices, overdue accounts receivable files and any other documents that need to flag your attention. Many bail agents require the defendant to come to the office 24 hours after he is bailed out so the bondsman can take the defendant's picture and have the defendant fill out personal information about himself. The additional information and photo are often helpful if the defendant skips. I have a designated file holder on my desk for defendants I'm waiting to see. If they don't show up, I will find their file and start calling and insisting that we make arrangements to meet.

If a defendant skips, you need to be able to find his file immediately. This means that if you bailed out 300 people this past year, you should have 300 files somewhere in your office – preferably in a filing cabinet, filed in a logical sequence. If any of those 300 defendants were to skip, you should know exactly where to locate his file, and you should be confident the file contains all the information and documents you need to track him down. The more detailed your filing system is, the more likely you are to complete your paperwork and have the information and documents readily available when you need them. And the more likely you are to stay on top of open cases, forfeitures and accounts receivable.

2. Create a procedure for handling new client calls.

It's not enough to have a good filing system in place. You need to use your filing system consistently and efficiently. The best way to do this is to have a specific game plan for processing new clients.

You should know exactly what needs to happen every time you decide to accept a new client. For every new bond I write, I know that I receive documents in a certain order and copy them in a specific way. I know exactly what paperwork needs to be completed and how, and I know where to file each piece of paper.

The easiest way to follow an organized procedure is to create a checklist. This will prevent you from overlooking important steps and ensure your paperwork is complete and accessible. As you grow accustomed to the procedure, you won't need to rely on the checklist as often. However, the checklist is a good practice to maintain, no matter how many bonds you've written. If you become busy and overwhelmed and tempted to cut corners, the checklist will keep you honest and on track.

3. Stay on top of open cases.

When you have defendants out on bail, you need a system for keeping tabs on them continually. You need to know where they are and what they're doing. Remember that court cases can take months to resolve. Even if you write just 10 bonds on average each month, after six months, half of those cases will likely remain open. That means you have 30 defendants out on bail and you're continuing to write new bonds. You should have a system in place that allows you to keep track of a defendant's court dates and to confirm that they showed up and fulfilled their obligations to the court. You should be on top of forfeitures and exonerations. Rather than simply bailing out defendants, putting their file in a cabinet and forgetting about them, set a reminder for yourself to follow up. For a defendant I bail out today, most likely his court date will be set 30 days from now. I set a reminder six weeks from now to call the court, check to be sure the defendant showed, and find out if the case is closed and the bail exonerated, or if another court date was set. If the bail was exonerated, I can mark in my records that the case is closed and return any collateral. When those steps are completed, I can archive my file.

Other procedures might work better for you. You can require that your defendants call you after every court date, set a reminder and then if you don't hear from them, you can call the court and find out what's going on.

Just because a defendant doesn't call, that doesn't mean he has skipped. He might have been sentenced and is now sitting in jail, unable to call. By checking with the court, you will find out what transpired. You can make it a habit to call the courts once or twice a week to check on the status of each defendant you have in court that week. Some courts have an online presence, so it's not always necessary to call – you can obtain the information you need over the Internet. Some bail agents have their clients call every Friday. Others set a reminder to check on their defendants every three or four months.

Some clients you won't be so worried about, while others you'll want to stay on top of. You might want to create a watch list of clients you're worried about and follow up with them more frequently. Sometimes the clients will notify you of their status, particularly if the bail is exonerated and they want their collateral returned.

You need to find a balance between how much time you spend tracking open cases versus how much time you devote to marketing your business and writing new bail. You don't have to call your defendants all the time, like a switchboard, but you also don't want to dump your files into a cabinet and forget about them. If you wrote a $10,000 bail bond for someone, just treat it as if he was walking around with $10,000 of your money. You need to keep tabs on where your money is. When a defendant skips, you have a limited amount of time to find him – the length of time varies by state – before you're required to pay the forfeited bond. Also, the more time that passes after a defendant skips, the more difficult it will be for you to locate him. If you aren't on top of where your defendants are, you might not be aware of forfeiture until it's too late to act.

If, on the other hand, you check continually on your defendants and have a system in place for following up, you will know what's going on with each of them. If they skip, you'll find out quickly enough when you still have time to act. If you're going to invest the time to write bail in the first place, the least you need to do is invest a little more time to follow up on each open case.

There are only two types of notices I receive from a court: exonerations and forfeitures. When I see a forfeiture in the mail, I panic as I'm opening it. When I see an exoneration, I am very happy. It's worth the time and effort to minimize the number of forfeiture notices you receive, and when you do receive them, you'll be glad you stayed on top of the situation so you can act quickly.

4. Keep a close watch on accounts receivable.

You need to know who owes you money, how much and what your payment arrangements are with each client. While this is common business sense, it's easy to overlook this task when you're busy. Someone might hand you a post-dated check, and you toss it in his file and forget about it. The check won't do you any good when you find it six months later. Meanwhile, the client thinks he has already paid you. If you make arrangements for someone to pay you every Friday after he receives his paycheck, and you are supposed to meet him in person to get the money, be sure you are not late. It is easy to forget appointments like this when you're busy, but if you're not there the day the client receives his paycheck, you're likely to have to wait another two weeks to see any money from him. He will have already spent it by the time you reschedule the appointment. I keep all my collection files on my desk as a reminder. I also have a database that tracks my accounts receivable and sends me reminders. But I still like to see the physical file on my desk so I know I won't forget.

It's best to limit your accounts receivable. When a person is still in jail he will jump through burning hoops to get out. That's the best time to have the client pay your premium -- preferably in full. If payment arrangements are necessary, that is also the best time to make those arrangements. Once the defendant has been released from jail, the urgency of the case has gone and you will be lucky to get the person on the phone, much less get them to agree to any type of arrangement.

Whatever payment arrangements you make with your clients, if you don't stay on top of your accounts receivable, they won't be of any use. You might as well be working for free.

5. Automate your systems as much as possible.

If someone called to say, "You bailed me out, and I forgot my court date," how quickly would you be able to find that person's information? If you asked them when they were bailed out, and they said, "I don't remember, I guess it was about two months ago," you would either have to look for that person's file or consult your ledger going back several months, searching for that person's name and information. Wouldn't it be easier if you could pull up that person's information instantly, while he is on the phone?

Several companies have designed software specifically for use by bail agents. You can enter all the relevant information that reflects the contents of your physical file folders, and you can access the information faster than sifting through stacks of documents. Some bail agent software programs even allow you to track accounts receivable.

If you type "bail bond software" into an Internet search engine, you will pull up a list of companies that offer this type of software, including:

- Creative Software Solutions
  (http://www.bailbondsoftware.com)

- Sentry Link, producers of Bail Credit
  (http://www.sentrylink.com)
- Bail Tracker 2000 by National Surety Services
  (http://www.bailbonding.com/software)
- BailBond Professional by Trackum Software
  (http://www.bondsmansoftware.com)

Software products range in reliability and features, so ask to see a demo to evaluate the software before you purchase it. It's also a good idea to find out how long a software company has been in business and ask for testimonials before investing in software. You don't want to find yourself without technical support if the software company goes under after a few months. The cost of bail agent software programs ranges from $500 to several thousand dollars. If you don't want to invest that much, you can create your own database using Microsoft Access. Whatever type of automated system you decide to use, remember that the system is only as good as the information you put into it. If you don't keep your software files updated, you won't be able to access the information you need.

Software does not replace physical file folders. You still need to keep originals of important documents. The length of time you are required to keep your archived files varies by state – in California it's five years – but it's a helpful business practice to keep them as long as possible. You never know when you'll want to refer back to information from an old case. If a defendant never paid your complete premium, for example, and now he's back in jail several years later, you'll want to require his overdue payment and current payment up front before you agree to bail him out again.

6. Hire help if needed.

If you are falling too far behind in your paperwork and administrative tasks, you might need to hire help. This doesn't necessarily mean that you need to take on a permanent full-time employee. You can hire temporary help – someone to come in and help you catch up on your paperwork. If you're too busy on a regular basis to stay on top of filing, you can hire a part-time employee to come in for one or two hours a day or several days a week and file or make follow-up calls. Hiring office help will increase your expenses and liability – as discussed in the next chapter. But if you continue to fall behind in your organizational tasks, hiring an office assistant might be worthwhile or even necessary. As you allow work to pile up, you run the risk of increasing your expenses and liability more than if you hired a part-time assistant. Compare the risk and expense of hiring part-time help versus allowing a forfeiture to slip through the cracks unnoticed, and you'll probably decide it's a better investment to hire help.

The more thought you put into planning your organizational systems and the more procedures you put into place, the better off you'll be. If you are organized, you will know exactly what steps to go through with each new client file: where and how to retrieve critical data and documents quickly, how to flag documents or accounts that require your immediate attention, and how to stay on top of defendants' court appearances so you won't be caught off-guard by a forfeiture notice.

6

MANAGING YOUR AVAILABILITY

People are arrested all the time. If you want the job of bailing them out, you need to be available all the time – whether or not you have an office, and whether or not you are in your office when the calls come through. I have written bonds on Christmas Day and Thanksgiving Day and every other holiday. In fact, I've written bonds every day of the year over my career. This includes vacation days. I've spent time on the beach in Hawaii, on vacation, negotiating bonds back in California, trying to work out details via fax and posting through my surety company. I've also developed a relationship with other bail agencies, so that if I get a call when I'm out of town and can't post the bond, I can at least earn a referral fee.

It's taxing, especially when you don't have employees, to handle incoming calls 24 hours a day, seven days a week, but if you are going to remain competitive in this business, you just have to work out some arrangement. If you are not available you will lose calls and consequently lose business. To succeed as a bail agent, you need to accept that you must be available, in one way or another, every hour of every day throughout the year.

When phones are down, business is down

When I first started in this business I wasn't as diligent with my availability as I am now. I would turn my phone off after 11:00 p.m., until a colleague pointed out that wasn't advisable. What if a call came through at 11:01 p.m. and I missed the opportunity to earn $1,000 or perhaps even $10,000? When you are trying to grow a business, you need to be available all the time. You can't afford to lose incoming calls.

You never know when an important call will come in
A bail agent will receive only so many calls a month, and it's not possible to know when the next call will come in. If you don't have a way to capture all incoming calls, you will lose out on potential business. Even worse, you will feel pressured to write bail for every one of the calls that you do receive – you may end up writing risky bail. Even if you try to keep your phone on around the clock, if you're trying to operate your bail bond business by yourself with just one phone line, you are going to miss a lot of calls. A new call might come in while you are on the line with another client, and if you have just one phone line, you'll miss it. The client won't call back. If you don't answer his call the first time, he will move on to the next bail agent in the phone book. Don't count on voice mail to help you either—by the time you return the call the defendant will probably have found another bail agent. Remember that defendants do not want to sit in jail any longer than they have to, so they are not going to wait around until it is convenient for you to take their calls.

To succeed in this business, you have to be prepared to take incoming calls around the clock. You need a reliable system in place to capture all incoming calls live, and you need to learn how to juggle and prioritize calls. Otherwise, you will lose too many opportunities and soon be out of business.

Learn how to win business

It is not enough just to answer the phone every time it rings. You have to learn how to engage and negotiate with clients so that you win their business and so they don't hang up and move on to the next bail agent listed in the phone book. You have only a few minutes to capture them, and if your technique is not effective and you lose the call, you might as well not have answered the phone in the first place.

Many new agents make the mistake of answering a client's questions too abruptly.

For example, typically, a client wants three questions answered: **"What does it cost?" "Do I need collateral?"** and **"When can you get him out?"** If all you do is tell the client your premium and say, "Yes, you need collateral," the call will end before the client even asks the third question. He will go on to the next bail agent in the phone book, searching for the bondsman that sounds nicer or a little more helpful on the phone or says what he wants to hear — that he doesn't require collateral. Instead you want to keep the person on the line and give them a stake in working with you. If the client says, "I need a bond for $10,000; what do I do?" a smart bail agent will say, "Which jail is the person in?" "How much is the bail?" and "Do you know what he was arrested for?" That keeps the client engaged in conversation with you. At that point, the client might start saying, "He's innocent. He didn't do it." Then you take the conversation in a different direction. Ask the client, "What time did the arrest take place?" He'll either give you an answer or say he doesn't know, and he'll probably then ask if you can find out more for him.

That's your cue to say, "I'll check the jail, get all the information you need and call you back right away." The client will give you his name and number and he will proceed to close the phone book, because he is now waiting for your call. As long as you call him back right away, you've more than likely captured his business. For many of the people who call you, this is their first time dealing with a bail agent. They aren't sure how things work or what to do. Rather than simply answering their questions, you need to address their needs. Take a friendly approach. Explain things patiently. Give them confidence in you so that they feel you'll be able to help them. I have a spiel that I go through that answers the three typical questions – premium, collateral and time until the defendant is released from jail – before the client even asks the questions. By the time I'm done with my 30-second spiel, the client has his answers and understands how the bail process is going to work. Then I ask him a few questions, which gives him an indication that I'm competent. At that point, the client usually says, "Where do we go from here?" and I tell him what the next step will be.

Every time a client calls, you have an opportunity to capture that client's business. If all you do is let him ask his three questions and then answer in monosyllables, you're not doing your job. You risk losing business that way. There is so much more you can do in those 30 seconds. If your competitor sounds better on the phone and has better things to say, he will be the one writing the bond instead of you.

Where does the trouble start?

It's tempting for new bail agents to limit their incoming calls and availability – either to keep down their costs or to maintain a more relaxed schedule. They forget that incoming calls represent new business. The only way to grow your business is to answer the phone.

How will you manage your time?

When you start out in this business, you need to decide how much time you are willing to commit to it. If you want to work 9 to 5, just a few days a week, the bail industry probably isn't right for you. But if you're committed to working as a bail agent and just want to limit your hours so you are not taking calls around the clock, you need to make arrangements to keep your business going around the clock, even when you are not available. This can include developing a relationship with another bail agency that is open 24 hours a day and arrange to forward your incoming calls to them for a referral fee. Or, you can hire a 24-hour answering service or another employee. But simply turning off your phone, with no forwarding arrangements, is not a good business practice. It's the same as shutting down your business, and if you do it too often, you'll soon be shutting down permanently.

Taking calls at night

Some bail agents feel secure turning off their phone at night, because they are building their business mostly on attorney referrals. Attorneys call mainly during daytime hours.

But these agents take a risk by turning off their phones at night. While you can manage to stay in business with several attorney calls per month, you take a chance by depending solely on attorney referrals. Months might go by when they don't call, and you will need to find or depend on other sources for new business. Moreover, attorneys might stop referring to you if you're not available 24 hours a day. Just because attorneys work mostly daytime hours doesn't mean they won't refer clients to you who may call you at night. If clients complain to an attorney that you're not taking their calls, the attorney might get annoyed and find another bail agent to whom he can refer clients. This doesn't mean you have to take the calls personally at night. As long as you have your calls covered around the clock by someone the clients will be satisfied and won't be likely to complain to the attorney.

Covering calls on vacation

If you decide to leave your phone on all the time, there will be times when you've put in such a long day that you will need to take an evening off. Even if you're a workaholic, you'll want to take some vacation time every year so you don't burn out.

Before you take time off, make sure that your incoming calls will be covered and that you have someone – an employee or another bail agent with whom you have a referral arrangement – who can write bail and follow up on clients in your absence. You still might want to maintain at least some availability while you're on vacation in case an urgent problem arises.

Warning signs

To keep your business growing steadily, be sure to have sufficient availability. Don't put yourself in a position to miss that next important call. When a bail agent isn't available enough for new clients, there are clear warning signs. Learn to recognize these so you can stay on top of your availability. Ask yourself the following questions:

1. Is your phone system too limited?

If you're afraid to tie up your phone line by taking too long on a call or afraid to leave your office because you might miss a call, you need to implement a better phone system. Multiple lines, call waiting and call forwarding are essential phone features for bail agents who want to grow their business. Cell phones, pagers and answering services provide even more flexibility to help you grow your business. You can find a reliable system that fits within your budget.

2. Are your business hours too limited?

If you don't have some type of phone coverage 24 hours a day, seven days a week, your business hours might be too limited. By its nature, the bail industry doesn't observe an eight-hour business day or a five-day workweek. Arrests happen all the time. If you are there to write bail when it's needed, you will find plenty of clients to keep your business going.

3. Do you have a good backup system in place?

What happens when you need to take time off – for vacation, or when you simply want to turn your phone off for one evening? Is someone else covering for you? If the answer is no, you could be losing valuable business. Suppose you turn your phone off one night and you miss a call for a $100,000 bond. If it was good bail, you've just lost the chance to earn $10,000 – in exchange for just one evening off. This doesn't mean you can't take an evening off —just have someone else available to answer calls in your absence.

4. Do you depend too much on employees or other agencies?

An office employee or two can be very helpful in keeping your business going 24 hours a day. Likewise, if you have a referral arrangement with another bail agency, you have someone to take your incoming calls in case you want to limit your evening hours or take time off. But if you're not careful you can become too dependent on others to handle your calls.

Employees are there to free up your time so you can write more bail and grow your business. They aren't there to cover your work for you so that you can take more time off. And while referral income from other bail agencies can be a nice supplement to your own income, it doesn't take the place of spending your time marketing and writing good bail.

5. Do you turn off your phone too frequently?

If you have developed a habit of turning off your phone nearly every day because you want uninterrupted free time, you need to rethink your business strategy. If you miss just one call for a $10,000 bond every time you turn off your phone (which can happen on a daily basis), you could be losing the chance to earn an extra $7,000 in premiums every week. If you have high overhead costs, that extra income could be critical. If you are tired of answering new calls all the time or feel that you're burning out, either hire another bail agent to share the workload, take a vacation, or align yourself with another bondsman. Take some time to step back and reassess your strategy. Perhaps you've been growing too quickly and can scale back a little so you won't feel so pressured.

How to avoid trouble

To be successful in the bail industry, you need to be available at all times to receive new business. While it's important to recognize the warning signs of limited availability, it is always best to be proactive from the start. Here are some steps you can take to be sure you are operating at optimum availability:

1. Have phone coverage 24 hours a day, seven days a week.

You need a good phone system in place: multiple phone lines with call waiting and call forwarding at a minimum, and a 24-hour answering service or in-house office assistance if necessary. An answering service is sometimes nice to have when you're just starting out, because you will always have someone answering your calls live. They can keep callers on the line while they try to reach you. In most office spaces, you can get a nice business phone system with five lines on it. Incoming calls will keep rolling over to the next line. If you work out of your home, you can install a multiline system, but it will be more expensive, as you'll need to rewire. And if you work alone, it might be difficult to manage more than two lines at once. To manage more than two lines, you might need to hire assistance.

Learn to assess incoming calls

Even with two lines or with call waiting, you need to learn how to juggle incoming calls. If I have two calls coming in at once, I'll answer both and try to evaluate which of the two is more important; that is, which one has a higher likelihood of working out or turning out to be good bail.

If a father is calling to bail out his son and at the same time a woman is calling about her drug-dealing boyfriend, I have a sense that the father-son situation will turn out to be better bail. So I'll tell the woman that I'll call the jail to get information on her boyfriend and call her back in 15 minutes. Then I'll have my wife call the jail and obtain the information while I make bail arrangements with the father calling about his son. If, when I call the woman back, she's already found another bondsman to bail out her boyfriend, it's not a huge loss. I won the other client, and it will probably prove to be better bail. And by taking down the woman's information and offering to call her back, I've cleared up the second phone line so another call can come through – possibly a better bail situation.

Cell phones and pagers are important

You also need one or more reliable cell phones so that your answering service or call forwarding can reach you when you're out of the office. Be sure you have a cell phone that has good reception. If your cell phone doesn't work well in certain locations consider getting two phones with different carriers. If one isn't working in a particular area, the other one might. Make sure your cell phone is on 24 hours a day. There's no sense in ever turning it off. If you do, it has to be a conscious decision knowing that you might lose business while your phone is off. It's also a good idea to have a pager because if you have to go to court, you won't be permitted to keep your cell phone turned on.

Instead, you can keep your pager on vibrate mode and people can reach you that way. Or if you have to go to the jail, you probably won't be able to use your cell phone. It might work in the lobby, but if you have to go inside to interview a defendant, you might not be permitted to bring your cell phone in. You might be asked to leave it in your car or in a locker. Even if you are permitted to carry it with you, you won't get a signal inside the jail. Pagers operate on a different system, however, so you can still be paged inside. It's probably not a good idea to include your pager number on your advertising, because you'll never know who you're calling back. But you can put it on your business card that you give to clients, attorneys and anyone else that refers business to you. That way they can always reach you. For all other calls, if you hire an answering service, they can place a caller on hold and punch in your pager number.

If you hire employees, it's useful for them to carry cell phones and pagers too. If you're negotiating a bond with a client and you know the situation is going to work out, you can call or page one of your employees to go write the bail while you stay in the office and handle other calls. Whatever type of phone system you put in place, be certain your equipment and service are reliable and always have a backup plan in case your power or service goes out, e.g., you can have your answering service forward all calls to your cell phone. You may even want to keep a land-line phone available to use in the event your power is out. Remember, if your phone system is down even for a short while, your business is also down.

2. Be ready for action.

Your success in this business depends on your willingness to keep your phone on 24 hours a day. Sometimes you will have to take calls when it's least convenient. Dinners will be interrupted, you'll be awakened in the middle of the night, you'll visit the jail on holidays, and you might need to negotiate bail while you are away on vacation. While this doesn't mean you'll be working around the clock, it does mean that you will have to be available at all times.

Be sure you can be reached

When you leave your office, your cell phone needs to be on. Your answering service needs to be able to reach you. It's not enough to rely on your pager whenever you're out of the office. A pager works well for situations when you can't use your cell phone, but it should never be your primary method of contact outside the office. If the answering service can't keep the caller on the line while they page you, by the time you call the client back he will have found another bail agent.

If I'm playing basketball, I have my cell phone turned on right next to the court. When I go to a movie, my phone is on vibrate mode, and I keep it in my lap so I can see when the light comes on. If it's the answering service, I need to go outside and call to see what's going on. In a restaurant where the signal might be weak, I keep the phone on the table next to my plate. I have a better chance of it picking up a signal there than in my pocket. I've answered the phone in the swimming pool and in the shower. I know I always have to do whatever is necessary to be sure I can grab the phone and answer. It is the nature of my work. As a bail agent, you won't be doing something every minute of every day. But you will always be mentally glued to the business. There might be sometimes when you just can't take a call and have to turn off your phone to sleep, but if you don't leave your phone on most of the time, you won't succeed in this business. You'll just be missing too many critical calls.

The cost of missed calls

It's important not to underestimate the randomness of incoming calls in this business. If you miss just one call, it might have been a big one. Depending on your current financial situation, the call you miss might have made the difference between covering your overhead expenses for the month or feeling forced to write risky bail to meet your expenses.

I remember one time when I was out surfing for two hours and I missed a call. By the time I got the message and called back, the bail had already been written by a competitor. The call I missed was an entire community bailing out someone for $25,000. I could have earned $2,500. That was the most expensive surfing session I've ever had. Fortunately I didn't have much overhead at the time so the missed call didn't threaten to put me out of business. But if I did have a lot of overhead, I'd have been in trouble. That $2,500 might have been critical, and I might not have received another call like that for another week or two.

Be prepared to move quickly

In the bail business, you also need to be ready to go out at a moment's notice. If a call comes in and it's for good bail, you need to be ready to drop what you're doing and go meet the client or go to the jail. You also need to be prepared to show up in court at a moment's notice. Sometimes an attorney will call you at 8:00 a.m. and say he needs you to be in court in half an hour. It's a good idea to keep a change of clothes in your car, including a suit for court. If you're at the beach in a T-shirt and flip-flops and a call comes in directing you to be in court in half an hour, you won't necessarily have time to go home and change. Or if you're at the gym and a call comes in for good bail with a client who's ready to meet you, it's helpful to have clean clothes on hand. You need to assume that every call is going to be somebody who needs you to go somewhere immediately – in the opposite direction of your house.

3. Know when you really need time off.

In this business you will have a tendency to want to be glued to your phone. All you want to do is answer the next call, write bail and make money. People need you and you want to be available for them at all hours of the day. Unfortunately, your business practice might prevent you from being available to your family and to yourself. The job can get to you after a while if you're not prepared. Being constantly available and not knowing what's going to happen next can be stressful. It's not just being available all the time, either. It's being available right then and there and ready for anything. Too many agents underestimate what it takes to be successful. The stress and the continual focus on writing bail lends itself to an unhealthy environment. The job takes away from the balance you need in life spending time with your family or just relaxing. I know too many bail agents who don't bother taking time out or engage in sports because they are afraid that they won't hear the phone ring or won't be able to reach it in time to take the call. Or they are afraid that the call will disrupt the game or that the client will hear the background noise and that the conversation will be difficult.

By not taking time out to engage in exercise, their health starts to deteriorate, and that makes it even harder for them to put in the long hours needed in this business. If you let the stress of the bail bond business affect your health it will not only become more difficult to handle the workload but you will also stop making good decisions. Your judgment will get clouded and you may start writing risky bail either because you're not thinking clearly or because exhaustion or stress has led you to mismanage your overhead costs until you become desperate for money.

It's important to take a step back before you let this happen. If you start to see warning signs of too much stress or fatigue, your immediate response should be to take time off before the situation becomes worse. Your next response should be to consider whether or not you need extra help – either hiring an employee or networking with another agency.

4. Network with other bail agents.

It's important to have a reliable network in place. Networking with other agents can keep your business going even when you need to take time off. You should always know what to do in any situation that might occur while you are out of the office. If you are out of the country and an attorney calls for a really big bond, you don't want to pass up that opportunity.

Not only do you want to grasp the chance to earn money on that bond, as you never know when you'll have such a big opportunity again, but you also don't want that attorney to call somebody else. If he is forced to call another agent this time, he might continue to refer clients to that agent in future. If you have a referral source with another agency you can always hand over the job to them while you are away. That way you are not losing clients. They still have your card and they know you are taking care of them. While they know you are working through a different company in this particular case, they also know that they can always rely on you to get everything squared away for them.

Referral arrangements for new business

Putting a referral arrangement in place when you first start out in this business will make it much easier to earn a profit. During my first year in business I earned roughly $20,000 by referring bonds to another company. That money made a huge difference in my ability to cover my advertising costs. The main reason I referred bonds was that I was concerned about taking risks. I didn't want to write questionable bonds, so I referred those clients to more established companies that were willing to write riskier bonds. That way, I still kept my relationship open with the clients and still earned a percentage, but without the liability. If you're new to the industry, call some other bail agents, attend the local bail association meetings and become involved in the statewide industry association. You can also ask your surety company to provide some names of local agents to whom you can refer business. Or you can open the phone book, call some of the agencies listed and introduce yourself. Tell them that you are new to the business, that you are still a very small operation, and that you are receiving a lot of calls for bail you don't want to write. Ask if they would like to enter into a referral relationship.

Too often, new bail agents are reluctant to give business to their competitors. It's a mistake. A small business can't survive without a network in any industry -- and that includes the bail industry. If you consider other agents as competition to be avoided, you'll miss out on a valuable resource.

5. Consider hiring agent employees.

If you're unable to keep up the pace or wish you could reduce your hours or take time off, it might be time to consider hiring one or more agent employees. Agent employees are different from the file clerk or receptionist you might hire to help you with office work. An agent employee can negotiate and write bail on your behalf. If you have an agent employee or two to run the business in your absence you can take a vacation without having to shut down your business temporarily or rely solely on referral income. You don't necessarily need to hire a graveyard employee to cover all the nighttime hours, just someone who will take the calls when you don't want to – to give you a break and to keep you from burning out.

Training employees

All employees you hire should be licensed as bail agents. It's important that you take the time to train them and set up some type of supervisory arrangement. I ask all my agents to run every new bond by me before they write it. I ask them to tell me exactly what's involved. I want to know everything about the client. I want to be the one to authorize the bond. That way if the bond is forfeited, I will be the one to blame, rather than my employees.

After a while your employees will have a sense of which bonds you would consider good and bad. They might be able to write good bail without your approval. However, it's always wise to have an authorization structure in place. For any bond over $1,000, I need to approve in advance, regardless of how good the bond looks.

If you don't keep some control over your employees and they start relying on their own discretion, they might become too relaxed. They are employees, not owners, and they don't carry your liability. Therefore, they might not consider risk in the same light as you would. It's helpful to have your employees fill out a client inquiry sheet with every bond they negotiate.

This prompts them to ask critical questions of the client and forces them to consider whether or not the bail is genuinely good. They can also research property and title information for collateral before running it by you. When you train your employees to follow your standard protocol with each client, you can feel confident that even though you didn't speak to the client, your employees asked all the questions you would have asked and did the research you would have done.

Some employees might require more training than others. They might not have a background in customer relations or they might lack marketing experience. If you have a particular spiel you use to handle phone calls make sure that the employee learns and uses the same spiel. If the employee lacks organizational skills, it's up to you to train him, to tell him, "this is the proper procedure to follow," and to make it clear that there will be no exceptions. If you don't take responsibility for training your employees and the job seems difficult to them, they will become easily discouraged or disgruntled.

Supervising employees

If you give your employees too much writing authority, combined with inadequate training and too little supervision, you can be asking for very big trouble. If they're frustrated or feeling overworked or underpaid, they won't pay careful attention to the work they are doing. They can write bad bonds without your knowledge. If your employees are too busy, they won't necessarily tell you. Instead they might be tempted to skip steps in the due diligence process. They might cut corners in completing paperwork and fail to file documents or follow up on open items. Whenever an employee decides to cut corners because he feels too overwhelmed, he risks writing bad bonds – and you will be liable for any forfeitures that occur.

One of my fellow agents had an employee that did a lot of cosigning by fax. Sometimes this is necessary, when a cosigner is in another state and the bail seems good. But it's not a good practice to get into. You lose the ability to "read" a client when you don't meet him in person. This particular agent wasn't cosigning by fax for people out of state. He was taking fax signatures from cosigners who lived just a few miles away because he felt he was too busy to meet them. Nor did he review the forms after they faxed them back. Some were not signed at all, and others contained incomplete or bad information. If any of those bonds had forfeited, the owner agent would have been liable for his employee's mistakes.

Fee-based arrangements

One way to keep employee agents from feeling overwhelmed and making mistakes is to pay them a fee based on every bond they write rather than put them on salary. Salaried employees know they will earn a certain amount regardless of the quantity of work they do. When they're busy, they'll pass the buck and not be interested enough to really negotiate with the client.

You can have two types of agent employees under this fee arrangement: one that puts in time in the office, negotiating and writing bail, and another that simply posts bail at the jail after you have negotiated. You might pay the in-house agent 10% of the premium on every bond he writes. This will encourage him to be savvier in negotiating with a client on a larger bond.

Meanwhile, you might pay the posting agent $50-150 every time he posts a bond at the jail. Both of these scenarios tend to be better than paying someone a flat salary. If you pay on a percentage basis and you have to authorize everything, your employees will try to obtain the right information so you don't reject the bond. It's in their best interest to choose good bail and be thorough so you'll approve and they haven't wasted their time. If they're on salary, on the other hand, they won't be motivated enough to do a good job when they become overwhelmed or frustrated. *(For a discussion on planning for employees, see Chapter 7.)*

Finding a balance

When you first start out, it takes a while to learn how to find a balance in managing employees. How much supervision is too little and how much is too much? You can't look over their shoulders every minute. For one thing, you wouldn't be getting your own work done, and you would probably drive them up the wall – or out the door. But you need to supervise them enough to be sure that, even with the best of intentions, they are not creating unnecessary liability for you. If you can find the right balance, employees can really benefit your business. If you're not sure how to manage them or how to establish their compensation structure, seek advice from more established businesses or from your accountant. If you have difficulty finding the right employees, don't give up. There are plenty of potential employees out there who will work well with you. Referrals from people you trust are sometimes the best way to find good employees.

7

WRITING A BUSINESS PLAN

One way to avoid all of the problems discussed in this book is to write a simple business plan. It's the most basic step in setting up a new business, but it's one that most bail agents – and most small business owners – overlook unless they are forced to prepare one because they are trying to secure start-up capital.

A business plan isn't something you write just for potential investors or loan officers. It's something every business owner should write and periodically update just for himself. It will help you avoid many mistakes and grow your business more effectively by enabling you to set out concrete goals, put systems into place and track your progress. You'll have something to measure every decision against so that you can determine whether the decisions you are making have been good or bad for the business.

Many bail agents believe writing a business plan is a luxury. This is wrong. A business plan is a necessity. If you don't have a roadmap for growing your business, how will you know if the next decision you make is good or bad? How will you be able to tell when you're moving in the wrong direction? A good business plan will give you all the answers you need, when you need them.

Where does the trouble start?

You might think a business plan takes too much time or effort to write when you are first starting out. You'd rather start advertising, answering incoming calls and writing bail. You may be tempted to think that you can always go back and write a business plan later, after your business starts to take off. The problem is that once your business takes off, you'll forget about writing a business plan. Or, you'll think you have no time for it. And as long as business is going well, you'll assume you don't need a plan.

That assessment will change the minute you get into trouble. You'll realize you have no plan of action and you desperately need one. At that point, it might be too late to go back and create a business plan. If it's not too late, it will at the very least be difficult to set a good plan in motion while you are stuck in a bad situation. You would have been much better off taking the time to write the business plan at the beginning.

If you don't take the time to write a business plan when you start your business, you won't have a clear sense of how much start-up capital you really need, what you can and should spend on advertising, how much growth you can manage, what type of infrastructure and staffing support you'll need and when, and how any given expenditure will affect your cash flow. You'll quickly find yourself overextended or under-equipped on advertising, office space and equipment, employees, business hours or available capital.

This is not a good way to run a business – especially not a bail business, where risk and liability can catch up to you at any time. No matter how busy you are, you can't afford not to take the time to write a solid business plan.

Warning signs

How does a bail agent know when he lacks a good business plan? When his business decisions result in unexpected and adverse consequences. A solid business plan provides decision-making guidelines and growth strategies. Without a plan, you can't assess the impact of every decision. The following are some of the problems that can result:

1. Lack of start-up capital.

If you are opening your own bail bond business, you will need start-up capital. Aside from whatever capital or collateral your surety company might require before they agree to back your business, you will also need enough money to invest in the basics: phones, fax, computer, office supplies and business cards. If you already have these essentials and plan to work from home to limit your initial costs, you will still need to pay for advertising. Without sufficient start-up capital to cover your advertising costs for the next six months, you might find it difficult to stay on top of your expenses. As we discussed before, you will be tempted to write risky bail just to earn enough to pay your advertising bills and office rent. Do you have a way to cover your overhead costs for the next six months, without resorting to writing risky bail? What if you don't receive enough calls this month or next month to cover your expenses? What will you do? If you don't have a good answer, or if you resort too often to writing bail just for the premiums you need to cover your bills, you stand to benefit by writing a business plan.

2. Lack of a budget.

If you don't have a budget, you have no way to know what you can or can't afford. As a bail agent, you might need to put down money for what you consider important items: yellow pages advertising, software programs, a consultation with an attorney or accountant, office space, an answering service or an employee. While each of these items is important, if you don't have a budget, you don't know what impact these expenditures will have on your business. What if you sign up for a billboard ad, hire an employee and order an expensive software program in your second month of business? You are assuming these investments will help you so much in expanding your business that they will pay for themselves within a month or two. Do you know that for certain? Do you know how you'll make up those costs if your phone doesn't ring much during the next two months and too few good bail opportunities come through the door?

If you don't know whether or not you can afford items that are essential or helpful to your business, or how and when you'll be able to pay for them, or if you have to resort to writing risky bail just to cover essential expenses, you need a business plan.

3. Lack of cash flow.

It's not enough just to cover your expenses from one month to the next. If your bail bond business is going to grow, you need to be earning a steady profit. You need continuous and predictable cash flow, so you know how, when and where you can expand your business. If you don't have a handle on start-up capital and budget issues sooner or later you will have trouble with cash flow. Bail agents sometimes forget they need cash flow not only to pay their bills, but also to expand their business and to set money aside for slow months. Additionally, when you own a bail bond company, you need to be able to pay yourself a salary so that you have an income to cover your personal obligations such as your mortgage, car payments and family care. Without reliable cash flow, you won't be able to pay yourself consistently. When personal financial pressures combine with business financial pressures, you'll be doubly tempted to write risky bail just for the premiums.

How are you going to generate sufficient cash flow during your first year of business to cover your costs, pay yourself and expand your business? If you don't know the answers a business plan can help you determine the best way to manage your cash flow.

4. Premature acquisition of office space.

While you can run a bail agency out of your home, having an office near the jail or courthouse can bring in a significant amount of walk-in traffic. This might be a good move for your bail bond company—if you can afford it. Unfortunately many new bail agencies acquire office space even though they can't afford it, and it's one of the biggest reasons companies go out of business in their first year. When you are just starting out, acquiring office space might be a premature decision. Even if you have the start-up capital to cover the initial expense, do you have enough capital to pay your office rent during the slow months? Are you certain you can set aside that capital and that you won't need it for anything else? Do you anticipate being forced to write risky bail because you've acquired office space before you were ready?

While the walk-in traffic your office space generates might be enough to cover the rent, careful planning is the only way to be confident that you have all the bases covered. If you are not certain whether or not you are ready for office space, don't make the decision without first writing a business plan.

5. Premature hiring of employees.

Just as with office space, employees can also help you expand your business significantly. But as with office space, employees also come with costs. Hiring employees prematurely can create huge financial liability for you, particularly if you are not careful about the way you structure the employment agreement or contract. The only way to know whether or not you are ready to hire an employee is through consultation and planning. If you have hired employees already and you are not certain whether or not the benefit of their work outweighs the costs, you might have hired them prematurely. Or, you might have skipped an important planning step and made your decision without the appropriate guidelines. If you are not certain whether or not you need employees, what type of employees you should hire or what type of pay structure you should offer, you need a business plan to guide you.

6. Overextension on advertising.

Advertising too much, too quickly is one of the fastest ways for a new bail agency to go out of business. As we said before you may end up practically working for the phone company as a majority of your income will go to pay for your ads each month. At worst, you'll be locked into a contract you can't afford, you won't earn enough to cover your ads and you'll be tempted to write risky bail just to keep up with your advertising expenses.

While advertising is important in generating new business there is such a thing as overextending your promotion. You need to determine how much advertising is necessary versus how much is too much. The only way to determine how much advertising you need and how much you can afford is to develop a solid business plan.

7. Inability to monitor growth.

When calls are rolling in, business seems good. If you are constantly writing bail and earning huge profits, you may consider whether it is time to expand. Should you try to capture a larger geographic area or hire employees to write even more bail or set up office space to capture walk-in traffic? Should you concentrate on writing bigger bail? If your business is truly going well, you might well be ready to expand.

But in order to make a well-informed decision, you need all the facts. Is your business really going well or are you just really busy? Do you have the capital, the cash flow, the budget and the infrastructure to support your expansion goals?

Will the benefits of expanding outweigh the costs? If you get in over your head, will you find yourself tempted to write all bail that comes through the door, regardless of the risk, just to earn more premiums and cover your expenses? Is expansion something you really want to be involved in, and if so, what type of expansion is best for you?

If you don't know the answers to these questions, create a comprehensive business plan before you think any further about expansion.

How to avoid trouble

To avoid these problems, start your business with a solid plan. When you write your business plan, you don't need to follow a particular format, unless you're trying to secure funding. You simply need a document that allows you to outline items such as start-up capital, budget, office infrastructure, advertising, employees, cash flow, accounting practices and growth strategies. And do put it in writing. Writing your plan will help you stay focused and will make you more accountable.

After you've written your business plan, you need to make a point of reviewing it regularly. Your business plan will be the primary guide you consult before you make any important decisions. It will let you know whether or not you're staying on track and what changes you might need to make to get back on track. You can modify your business plan as your business grows and changes.

Too many bail agents jump into the industry thinking, "I'll just throw an ad in the phone book, wait for the calls to come in and soon I'll be wealthy." They calculate the amount they need to earn from that phone book to recoup their investment, and after they earn that amount, they expand to another phone book. They keep expanding their advertising that way, until they end up so far over their heads that it's too late to fix the problem.

Had they written a business plan at the beginning, they wouldn't have had that problem. They'd know exactly where to advertise, how much to spend, and what criteria they would need to meet before they could expand further. When you start your bail bond business, you need to set out concrete and realistic goals, a strategy for achieving those goals and a budget that allows you to implement your strategy. You don't need a huge amount of capital to start out. You just need to keep your immediate goals realistic. Later, when you are truly successful, you can expand your goals. If you don't have enough capital to achieve even modest short-term goals, plan how you will earn the capital, sensibly, before you become too aggressive with your business.

If you don't have enough capital put away to cover six months' worth of expenses to compensate for slow months, you need to limit your expenses to the capital you do have and plan to save your initial income so you can start to grow. Professional consultations can help you get on track when you're first starting your bail bond company. Consider hiring a CPA or a business attorney to discuss your business plan. The consultation won't be cheap, but it will pay off in terms of the valuable advice they will give you. They can help you avoid problems that might otherwise hurt your business. A CPA can also explain your tax liability so you know how your business decisions might affect your taxes and which deductions you can and cannot take and with what limits. Networking with other bail agents or consulting with friends that are experienced business owners or knowledgeable in marketing can also be valuable.

Before you write your business plan, and even after you've completed it, be sure to pay special attention to three major growth and planning areas that cause bail agents to go off track, expand too quickly and make poor decisions:

- **Phone book ads**
- **Office space**
- **Employees**

We've already looked at how each of these problem areas can put your business at risk. Now let's look at ways to incorporate this knowledge into your business plan:

Planning for phone book ads

As you may have realized by now, to judge by how many times I have mentioned it, the phone book is the main source for advertising in the bail industry. Each phone book comes out once a year, so depending on when you submitted your ad it might take several months for your ad to appear in the phone book. Most often you won't have to pay for the ad until it comes out. When it does, it probably won't pay for itself right away. You should expect to pay the cost of the ad for at least one to three months before you earn enough from the ad to cover that expense.

This is where new agents get into trouble and make one of several bad decisions:

- They put off paying the bill for their phone book ad for several months, and the amount due adds up.
- They get into the habit early on of writing risky bail to cover the expense of the phone book ad.
- They decide they need more new business to cover the cost of the ad, so they take out an ad in another phone book, thus increasing their monthly costs.

This is why it's advisable to have sufficient start-up capital available, to plan your marketing and growth strategy up front and to grow slowly and steadily.

If you plan to advertise in more than one phone book in your area, keep in mind that the publication dates are probably staggered. You don't have to put ads in all of them at once. Find out when each phone book comes out and the deadlines for submitting an ad. This way, you'll give the first ad a chance to pay for itself before you take out an ad in another phone book.

Pay attention to pricing

Price your ads carefully. A phone book ad can cost anywhere from $5 to $5,000 per month. You need to plan how much you want to spend per month on phone book advertising and choose your ads accordingly. If you take out the largest ad, you will have more exposure but you will spend a lot of money.

The line ads and small ads at the back of the section can pull just as well as a large ad on a percentage basis. While you might receive relatively fewer calls from a smaller ad, you'll be spending relatively less. That might be the best way to start out.

You can expand later, when you're ready and when advertising growth fits in with your business plan. This doesn't mean you need the smallest one-liner ad. You can take out a one-inch column ad for roughly $50-100 per month and you'll have decent exposure. You won't bring in as much business as you would with a large ad, but you will stand out from the one-line ads. You don't need anything much bigger at first. Wait until you know, according to your business plan, that you can afford it, and be sure it's a good strategic business decision.

How many ads are too many?

Business strategy isn't only important just when you are deciding the size of your phone book ad; you also need a sound strategy for determining how many ads to take out in how many phone books. The common mentality among bail agents is, "If I spend $100 per month on one ad, and that ad brings in an average of $300 per month, I'm earning enough to take out an ad in another phone book." If that second ad seems to be pulling its weight, the bail agent is tempted to take out even more ads.

When bail agents take out too many ads, it's because they haven't thought through the process. They haven't researched what works and what doesn't. They haven't considered the snowball effect. *They don't have a solid business plan.*

If you're expanding your advertising simply because you're able to cover your costs, you're not being strategic. You're not looking ahead to a time when you can't cover those costs. Meanwhile, you've become an employee of the phone company.

Compare spending $1,000 on phone book advertising to spending almost nothing by networking for attorney referrals – advertising that will almost certainly result in repeat business. Phone book ads certainly can earn you substantial business and income, and it's important to have a few yellow page ads. But when you are starting out in this business, consider the value of lower-cost advertising through attorney referrals. Make every single advertising decision part of a solid business strategy.

Planning for office space

When you own a bail agency, you can choose to work out of your home or in an office. Each scenario has its advantages and disadvantages. It's nice to be able to work out of your house rather than having to go to an office every day. But working from home presents challenges you need to consider.

Challenges of working from home

At home, you have to deal with distractions: kids playing, dogs barking, a lawn that needs mowing. Another problem with working from home is that sometimes it is hard to maintain a home life. Rather than coming home from your office to relax, you are in a sense living in your office.

Working from home can also present logistical problems. You can't have clients meet you at home. You don't know who these people are, and you don't ever want your clients to know where you live. Not being able to provide clients with an office address can be a problem sometimes. Some people have the misconception that bail bondsmen are criminals, and if you don't have an office address to give them, they might think you are not a legitimate business.

They'll be afraid that if you meet them at the jail or in a parking lot you are trying to scam them and they'll never be able to find you again. I've lost some business by working at home. But in most cases it is not a problem. I've met clients in parking lots, fast food restaurants, jails, police stations, courts, etc. I always try to look, act and dress professionally.

Even though it's not necessary to have an office, some bail agents prefer it. They don't like the distractions of working at home. They want to be closer to the jail, so they're not driving such a long distance back and forth between home and jail. Or they want a place where they can meet their clients and take care of paperwork comfortably.

Think carefully before investing in office space

Before you make the decision whether or not to have office space outside your home, you'll need to do some careful planning. Office space is not cheap, and usually you'll be locked into a one-year lease. If you don't have the business experience or cash flow to support these costs, you could find it difficult to keep up with your office rent. The last thing you want when you're starting out in this business is an unnecessary financial burden that tempts you to write risky bail. I have seen a lot of bail offices come and go. A company's sign goes up in an office window across from the jail. A few months later the sign is gone. Shortly after that another bail agency moves in and soon that agency, too, is gone.

Bail agents are attracted to office space across the street from jails. They put in big neon signs and big arrows pointing clients in their direction. This approach does work. An office near the jail can bring you walk-in business -- perhaps even enough to cover the rent on the office space. But to make the most of this prime location, you need to have your office open 24 hours, which means that you need an agent employee to run the office during the hours that you are not there.

Also, you need to be sure the agent stays awake so that when someone knocks on the door in the middle of the night, he will answer it. To successfully run an office across from the jail you also need to have your office staffed full-time during the day. Even if you have another agent employee, if one of you is across the street posting bail and the other is at a jail across town, who is at the office to handle walk-in traffic? If you close the office even for half an hour during the day and a client walks by during that time, you're losing business.

Unless you hire sufficient staff to have someone in the office at all times, you'll spend potentially thousands of dollars a month on office space and you won't get the walk-in traffic to justify the expense. The bail agencies that stay in business and manage to keep their offices are the ones that never lock their doors. Even if you can afford to hire employee it won't be easy to find people to work the graveyard shift. People might think they can do it at first but then they realize it's not that easy to work all night. And what happens if your night employee calls in sick? Will you be ready to cover those hours after you've worked all day – knowing that you have to turn around and work again the next day? Office space might be the right move for your bail bond company; but before you lock yourself into a lease, make sure your decision to acquire office space is the result of careful planning. Think through what it will take to keep your office open around the clock every single day of the year. Determine how you will cover your rent during slow months, without feeling pressured to write risky bail. Be sure you're choosing to have an office for the right reasons – and that your decision will benefit rather than harm your business.

Planning for employees

Even if you work at home and don't need employees to keep your office open 24 hours a day, you might need employees to help you manage your workload. Running a 24-hour business isn't easy—even without an office to maintain.

Challenges of working around the clock

As a bail agent, you'll want to be available around the clock. This means you might get a call at 3:00 a.m. and have to head out to the jail. You'll take care of business there, head back home, and the minute you get into bed, the phone rings again.

Are you ready to go back out? It might be all right if this happens once or twice a month, but if you have calls like this coming in twice a week, it'll start to take a toll on you. How much work can you really handle? What if you work until 11:00 p.m., come home, go to sleep and another call wakes you at 2:00 a.m.? That's hard enough under any circumstances, but what if you have to be in court first thing in the morning? Will you have to turn down the 2:00 a.m. client so you can get some sleep, or will you agree to go out and write the bail and hope you can stay awake in court the next day?

I've known many agents who started out thinking it would be no problem to work around the clock. They soon discovered it was more of a problem than they anticipated. Working too many hours is the fastest way to burn out, and when you're overly exhausted, you make poor decisions. Thus, it can be helpful to hire an employee to relieve some of the burden of long hours.

You don't need a full staff right away

This doesn't mean that you need to go out and hire an entire staff. You can start small and plan for your growth. It might be enough at first to pay a family member a little to help you out. Get them licensed as a bail agent so when you go out to write a bond or you are in court for two hours with no cell phone access, you'll know that they can handle the incoming calls.

They can either keep the caller on the line while they page you, or they can negotiate the bond and write it. You will capture more calls that way, which is important since you never know when another call will come in. If you're ready to hire employees, you don't need to hire them on a full-time salary basis. While some bail agents have salaried employees, these are usually the bigger and more established agencies. When you're starting out, you can hire employees on a contract basis and pay them a percentage per bond they write. This limits your costs and liabilities while providing you with assistance and the chance to write more bonds.

Learn the industry first

Before you hire agent employees, be sure you know how to do everything yourself. Too many bail agents neglect the important first step of learning the business. They just want to go out, write bail and hire employees so they can grow their business into a bigger company. They're not acting like professional owners. They are simply acting like investors. They want the profit without learning anything about the industry. If you're going to succeed you need to learn the business. You need to know what you're doing at all times and be prepared to learn from your mistakes. And you need to do this before you start expanding and hiring employees.

It is not advisable to jump into the bail industry for the first time and hire an employee right away. If you do, how will you train and supervise him? You need to have several years of experience in different situations so you can prevent your employees from getting into bad situations and increasing your liability.

Stay on top of liability

Even if you are careful to learn the business before hiring employees, they can still be a liability. If you don't screen your employees well, take time to train them, determine the best methods for paying and motivating them to write good bail and stay on top of their supervision. New, untrained employees can do a lot of harm in a short period of time. When they go out to write bonds on your behalf, you are giving them what amounts to a blank check in the full amount of each bond they carry. If your employees make bad decisions, you (not they) will be liable for the results. Not only might your employees write bad bail, but I have also known bail agents whose employees have engaged, willingly or ignorantly, in illegal activities, such as providing kickbacks to attorneys or inmates. I have known others whose employees have written bonds and pocketed the premiums. When they run out of bonds, they move on, and the bail agent is left without his premiums and with the full liability for each bond the employee wrote.

One way to keep track of your bonds and prevent this from happening is to write down the bond number of every bond you give your employees and have them sign a form indicating they have received that bond. You can also have them sign a legal agreement that holds them responsible for every bond in their possession and every bond they write. As the owner of the

115

agency you will still be held liable for any forfeitures. But this is a way to make your employees feel more responsible for their actions. If the surety company comes after you for a bad bond one of your employees wrote, you will be in a better position to go after your employee. Alternatively you can have your employees open a BUF account with you. You can take 10-20% of their income every month to deposit into the BUF account.

When an employee leaves your company, you can wait until all his bonds are exonerated and then return the money to him. When you hire employees, you not only have to be concerned with liability for the bonds they write. You also need to be sure they have full automobile insurance coverage and determine if you need any additional business insurance to cover them. An insurance expert and your business attorney can help you make these decisions.

Illegal practices

Poor planning is at the root of most problems that affect bail bond businesses. Lack of proper planning and the problems that result can cause bail agencies to go out of business. But there's another reason some agencies shut down: engaging in illegal practices. While I believe most new bail agents don't get into this business because they want to break the law, you should be aware of the problems illegal practices can cause. Be careful not to stumble into them inadvertently, and be sure to supervise your employees so they don't engage in these activities.

While attorney referrals are a valuable part of your business network, in most states you are not permitted to solicit attorneys at the courthouse. Instead, you need to meet with them in their offices. Nor are you allowed to give kickbacks to attorneys in exchange for new business. In most states, you're also not allowed to refer business to attorneys, although there are exceptions; in Texas, for example, some attorneys are bondsmen as well.

You're also not permitted to give kickbacks to inmates at the jail. Bondsmen sometimes pay inmates to hand out their name and number. If you are caught doing this, you will be out of business pretty quickly. Nor can you solicit new business at the jail. You can ask a client to tell others about you, but you can't pay him to do so. If he's happy with your services he'll likely refer you anyway. You can give your client your business card but be careful not to give out your business card to anyone else at the jail. Be aware that even wearing a T-shirt with your company's name on it can be considered solicitation when you are at the jail. You're also prohibited from commingling collateral and premium funds. Cash collateral needs to be accounted for separately and held in a designated trust account.

This is a bail industry requirement, and in California it's part of the state insurance code. If you deposit money, even inadvertently, into the wrong account, it can be considered theft. Bail agents get into trouble when they are having a slow month and they are tempted to use cash collateral deposits to cover their expenses. Not only will this practice make you vulnerable to legal action, but you will also put yourself at risk of not being able to repay the funds. If you're concerned about keeping your accounts separate, your surety company can open a trust account on your behalf at no cost to you. They can hold any cash collateral for you in that account. When you need to return the collateral to the client, the surety company will return it to you.

If you're caught engaging in any illegal act, you could have criminal charges brought against you. You could not only be fined heavily, but you could possibly face jail time. At the very least, you will lose your business and your bail agent's license. You won't even be able to work for another bail agency.

If one of your employees is caught engaging in illegal activities, the court will have to determine whether or not the action was taken under your orders or by his own initiative. Either way, it's not a good situation for you to be in, which is one reason it's so important to keep a close watch on your employees.

When you become licensed in your state, the licensing agency – typically the Department of Insurance – will explain what is and isn't legal practice. Some of this information will be included on your licensing exam. Be sure you take the time to learn it well, as it could mean the difference between running a successful bail bond company and getting into serious trouble.

In summary, take the time to *plan your business* well. Focus on slow and steady growth. Think through your decisions carefully. Gain some experience and cash flow before you expand your business too much. And be smart about advertising – don't turn over half your income to the phone company. If you plan well and stick to your plan, you will have a very good chance of running a successful bail bond business.

8

KEYS TO SUCCESS

If you commit to growing your bail bond company slowly and steadily, based on careful thought and planning, you can have a very successful business. Now that you're aware of the most common mistakes made by bail agencies that fail, let's review what you have learned from the mistakes of others. These are your keys to success:

1. Bail out the right people.

Remember how the bail process is supposed to work. It's not about earning premiums to grow your business quickly or get yourself out of a financial hole. It's about helping people fulfill their obligations to the court and writing bail only for defendants who seem dependable – a good risk. Focus on bailing out the right people for the right reasons and you will be off to a good start.

2. Complete your due diligence.

It's impossible to tell whether or not a defendant is a good risk unless you conduct thorough due diligence. Ask the right questions and pay close attention to the answers. Do background checks and title searches. If your due diligence raises or confirms doubts, decline the case or refer it on to another agency that handles riskier defendants.

3. Grow your business slowly and steadily.

You are in this business for the long-term. Don't race to corner the market. Keep your growth at a manageable pace. If you don't have enough start-up capital, work to accumulate it and keep your immediate goals realistic until you can afford to expand. If you concentrate on doing your job well, your company will grow over time. You will have a solid business with steady, reliable income and limited risk.

4. Stay on top of your paperwork.

As a bail agent you are legally required to maintain accurate and complete documentation on each client. That should be reason enough to keep your records up to date, but there's another reason: your business success depends on your paperwork. Fall behind, and you will face a higher risk of forfeitures, financial loss, and ultimately the end of your business. Stay on top of your paperwork, keep everything in good order, and you will operate a stable and successful business.

5. Be available around the clock.

Defendants are arrested 24 hours a day, seven days a week. If you aren't available to post bail at all times, you will lose out. Because you never know when the next client will call or walk in the door, think twice about turning off your phone or closing your office. Even if you're out of reach for an hour, you might miss an opportunity to write a $100,000 bond that doesn't come along very often. This doesn't mean that you have to work literally around the clock, just that you need to make arrangements – employees, referral networks – to have your business covered at all times.

6. Write a solid business plan – and stay on track.

Now that you've learned everything that can go wrong with a bail company – and how to anticipate and correct mistakes – it's time to write your business plan. With a solid business plan, you will have a reliable way to measure every decision you make. You'll know exactly how to grow your business, and if you get off track, your business plan will help you regain your focus. Before you go any further, take the time right now to draft a business plan. If you do, you can avoid all the mistakes discussed in this book. You'll be off to a very successful start.

RESOURCES

Websites

American Bail Coalition
http://www.americanbailcoalition.com
This website highlights laws pertaining to the bail bond industry in each state, including licensing fees and exam requirements.

Professional Bail Agents of the United States
http://www.pbus.com
This website describes the upcoming events and activities of this national bail association, as well as membership and networking opportunities and the latest news affecting the bail industry. The site also has links to many Statewide Bail Association websites.

Bureau of Justice Statistics
http://www.ojp.usdoj.gov/bjs
This is the official website of the Bureau of Justice Statistics, the government agency responsible for compiling numbers about anything pertaining to criminal justice in the United States. The website contains information concerning criminal offenders,

victims, law enforcement, prosecution, the federal court system, corrections, and other related topics.

Bail Referral Services and Directories

http://www.Bail.com A Nationwide Bail Bond Referral Service.

http://www.AboutBail.com A Nationwide directory of Bail Agents, Criminal Attorneys, Investigators and more…

http://www.BailBond.com A Nationwide directory of Bail Bond Companies, PI's and Attorneys.

http://www.PrivateInvestigatorDirectory.com A PI and Bail Enforcement Agent Directory.

Official state websites

To learn more about licensing requirements for bail agents in a particular state, visit the official website for the regulatory department in that state. Because each state's DOI or Department of Commerce handles many different topics, it's often difficult to find bail agent licensing information quickly. It is sometimes included with licensing information for other types of insurance agents, but even that can be hard to find. If your state's website has the bail agent information buried deep within, try the site's search function. Type in "bail bond" or "surety agent" or "bail bond license" to locate the appropriate section.

If all else fails, each site has a phone number or e-mail address for you to use to obtain more information.

<u>Following is a list of relevant state websites:</u>

Alabama

http://www.aldoi.org

Alaska

http://www.dced.state.ak.us/insurance

Arizona

http://www.id.state.az.us

Arkansas

http://www.arkansas.gov/insurance/

California

http://www.insurance.ca.gov

Colorado

http://www.dora.state.co.us/insurance

Connecticut

http://www.ct.gov/cid

Delaware

http://www.state.de.us/inscom

D.C.

http://www.disr.washingtondc.gov

Florida

http://www.fldfs.com

Georgia

http://www.inscomm.state.ga.us

Hawaii

http://www.hawaii.gov/dcca/ins

Idaho

http://www.doi.state.id.us

Illinois

http://www.ins.state.il.us

Indiana

http://www.in.gov/idoi

Iowa

http://www.iid.state.ia.us

Kansas
http://www.ksinsurance.org
Kentucky
http://doi.ppr.ky.gov/kentucky
Louisiana
http://www.ldi.la.gov
Michigan
http://www.michigan.gov/cis
Mississippi
http://www.doi.state.ms.us
Maine
http://www.state.me.us/pfr/ins/ins_index.htm
Maryland
http://www.mdinsurance.state.md.us
Massachusetts
http://www.state.ma.us/doi/
Minnesota
http://www.commerce.state.mn.us
Missouri
http://www.insurance.state.mo.us
Montana
http://www.sao.state.mt.us
Nebraska
http://www.nol.org/home/NDOI
Nevada
http://www.doi.state.nv.us
New Hampshire
http://www.nh.gov/insurance
New Jersey
http://www.state.nj.us/dobi
New México
http://www.nmprc.state.nm.us/insurance/inshm.htm
New York

http://www.ins.state.ny.us
North Carolina
http://www.ncdoi.com
North Dakota
http://www.state.nd.us/ndins
Ohio
http://www.ohioinsurance.gov
Oklahoma
http://www.oid.state.ok.us
Oregon
http://www.cbs.state.or.us/external/ins
Pennsylvania
http://www.ins.state.pa.us
Rhode Island
http://www.dbr.state.ri.us
South Dakota
http://www.state.sd.us/drr2/reg/insurance
South Carolina
http://www.doi.state.sc.us
Tennessee
http://www.state.tn.us/commerce
Texas
http://www.tdi.state.tx.us
Utah
http://www.insurance.utah.gov
Vermont
http://www.bishca.state.vt.us
Virginia
http://www.state.va.us/scc/division/boi
Washington
http://www.insurance.wa.gov
West Virginia
http://www.state.wv.us/insurance

Wisconsin
http://oci.wi.gov/oci_home.htm
Wyoming
http://insurance.state.wy.us

<u>Federal government website</u>
http://www.firstgov.gov
This is the official website of the U.S. government, and it's filled with information and resources. The section entitled "Laws and Regulations" contains links to searchable legal databases, a copy of the U.S. Constitution and other laws, information on how the court systems work, access to government publications and links to legal resources. That's only one segment of this extensive site. No subscription is required for this valuable resource – you've already paid for it with your tax dollars.

Book Resources

Bail Bonds 101: The Complete Guide to Owning and Operating a Successful Bail Bond Company. This is a comprehensive, detailed guide for Bondsmen. It is the first book of its kind for the bail industry. It can be found on www.bail.com or www.amazon.com.

Law Dictionaries

You might want to have access to a legal dictionary when you're just starting your bail bond business. You can find and bookmark numerous free websites listing legal terms, or you might want a simple pocket dictionary. *Merriam-Webster's Dictionary of Law* is only $12 in paperback, or *Dictionary of Legal Terms: A Simplified Guide to the Language of Law* by Steven H. Gifis is $9 in paperback.

If you're more serious about law, you can pick up *Black's Law Dictionary*, edited by Bryan Garner. This reference book is more detailed and includes the U.S. Constitution. It is $60 in hardcover, $25 in paperback.

Criminal Justice Guides

For a thorough academic view of our criminal justice system, try *Introduction to Criminal Justice*, 9th edition, by Joseph J. Senna. This detailed textbook explores the history, procedures, ethics, theories, vocabulary and other aspects of our criminal justice system. It's $75 in hardcover.

If you just want the basics, try *Law 101: Everything You Need to Know About the American Legal System* by Jay M. Feinman. It's only $20 in hardcover, and it covers the Constitution, civil law and procedure, contract and property law, criminal law and criminal procedure.

Accounting references

You might want to learn the basics of accounting to do the bookkeeping for your bail bond agency. Try *Accounting for Dummies* by John A. Tracy (a *For Dummies* publication) or *Small Business Accounting Simplified* by Daniel Sitarz (Nova Publishing). Both paperbacks sell for approximately $16 and are written for individuals with no formal background in accounting.

SEAN M. COOK

INDEX

A

accounting records, 61
accounts receivable, 33, 46, 63, 64, 65, 67, 68, 71, 72
advertise, 6, 56, 63, 105, 108
advertising, 6, 8, 17, 48, 50, 51, 52, 53, 55, 56, 85, 90, 98, 100, 103, 105, 107, 108, 109, 118
advertising costs, 51, 54, 100
agent employees, 91, 94, 114
answering service, 79, 83, 85, 86, 87, 100
attorneys, 55, 80, 85, 115, 116
availability, 5, 35, 76, 79, 80, 81, 83

B

background searches, 18, 44
backup system, 82
bad decisions, 9, 8, 13, 54, 107, 115
bail agents, 3, 6, 9, 2, 14, 15, 20, 25, 26, 27, 28, 30, 32, 35, 39, 48, 49, 52, 53, 54, 58, 59, 63, 66, 67, 69, 72, 79, 81, 89, 90, 91, 92, 96, 105, 106, 109, 110, 114, 115, 116, 123
bail bond, 3, 9, 2, 3, 4, 6, 8, 10, 12, 14, 15, 16, 22, 23, 27, 48, 52, 53, 56, 57, 61, 62, 65, 66, 70, 72, 76, 89, 100, 101, 102, 105, 106, 112, 116, 118, 119, 122, 123, 128, 129, 2
bounty hunter, 11, 18, 22, 35, 36, 59
budget, 6, 53, 55, 81, 100, 101, 104, 105
business plan, 5, 6, 8, 50, 96, 98, 99, 100, 101, 102, 103, 104, 105, 106, 107, 108, 109, 121

C

cash flow, 14, 15, 17, 20, 21, 63, 98, 101, 102, 104, 105, 111, 118
collateral, 3, 4, 7, 11, 12, 14, 19, 22, 23, 24, 25, 27, 28, 29, 31, 32, 34, 36, 38, 39, 40, 41, 42, 44, 57, 59, 60, 61, 64, 65, 66, 69, 70, 77, 78, 92, 100, 117
constantly available, 88
cosigner, 3, 4, 7, 14, 15, 19, 22, 23, 25, 26, 27, 30, 31, 37, 38, 40, 44, 57, 60, 66, 93
cosigning by fax, 93
costs, 6, 9, 17, 40, 48, 49, 50, 51, 53, 54, 55, 79, 83, 89, 90, 100, 101, 102, 103, 104, 107, 109, 111, 114

D

defendant skips, 9, 11, 15, 18, 22, 25, 35, 38, 40, 67, 70
Desperation, 6, 8, 47
disorganization, 64
due diligence, 5, 6, 7, 10, 14, 16, 22, 23, 25, 26, 27, 28, 29, 30, 31, 32, 33, 34, 36, 37, 39, 40, 44, 46, 47, 59, 60, 62, 93, 120

E

expenses, 6, 10, 14, 15, 17, 21, 24, 36, 46, 50, 53, 54, 55, 61, 74, 87, 100, 101, 103, 104, 106, 117

F

filing system, 58, 66, 67, 68
forfeit, 13, 31, 32, 36, 42, 57

ABOUT THE AUTHOR

Sean M. Cook has been in the bail bond business since 1992. While working for one of the largest bail companies in California, he gained extensive knowledge of the industry. A few years later, Sean ventured out on his own to open his bail agency, which he has success fully operated since 1995. Since then, he has acquired another bail agency and has the largest bail online presence with his website, **www.bail.com**.

Sean is considered a bail bond expert among bail professionals. He wrote this book because he has seen too many new bail agencies fail for reasons that could have been prevented. He is the author of *Bail Bonds 101: The Complete Guide to Owning and Operating a Successful Bail Bond Company* (CA: Bail Out Publishing 2005). Sean is an active member of Professional Bail Agents of the United States and the California Bail Agents Association. He lives in California.